MODERN
NATIONS
—OF THE—
WORLD

# SRI LANKA

## TITLES IN THE MODERN NATIONS OF THE WORLD SERIES INCLUDE:

Afghanistan
Algeria
Argentina
Australia
Austria
Belize
Bolivia
Brazil
Cambodia
Canada
Chile
China
Colombia
Congo
Costa Rica
Cuba
Czech Republic
Denmark
Egypt
England
Ethiopia
Finland
France
Germany
Greece
Guatemala
Haiti
Hungary
India
Indonesia
Iran
Iraq
Ireland
Israel
Italy
Japan
Jordan

Kenya
Kuwait
Lebanon
Liberia
Libya
Mexico
Morocco
Nicaragua
Nigeria
North Korea
Norway
Pakistan
Panama
Peru
Philippines
Poland
Russia
Saudi Arabia
Scotland
Somalia
South Africa
South Korea
Spain
Sudan
Sweden
Switzerland
Syria
Taiwan
Thailand
Turkey
United Arab Emirates
United States
Vatican City
Vietnam
Yemen

MODERN
NATIONS
—OF THE—
WORLD

# SRI LANKA

BY DEBRA A. MILLER

**LUCENT BOOKS**

*An imprint of Thomson Gale, a part of The Thomson Corporation*

THOMSON
———✳———™
GALE

Detroit • New York • San Francisco • San Diego • New Haven, Conn.
Waterville, Maine • London • Munich

THOMSON

™

GALE

On cover: A street scene in Kandy in the hill country of Sri Lanka.

© 2006 Thomson Gale, a part of The Thomson Corporation.

Thomson and Star Logo are trademarks and Gale and Lucent Books are registered trademarks used herein under license.

*For more information, contact*
Lucent Books
27500 Drake Rd.
Farmington Hills, MI 48331-3535
Or you can visit our Internet site at http://www.gale.com

LIBRARY OF CONGRESS CATALOGING-IN-PUBLICATION DATA

Miller, Debra A.
    Sri Lanka / by Debra A. Miller.
        p. cm. — (Modern nations of the world)
    Includes bibliographical references and index.
    ISBN 1-59018-626-5 (hard cover : alk. paper)
    1. Sri Lanka—Juvenile literature. I. Title. II. Series.
DS489.M45 2005
954.93—dc22

                                                                        2005010017

Printed in the United States of America

# CONTENTS

INTRODUCTION                                6
    Fall from Paradise

CHAPTER ONE                                11
    An Island Jewel

CHAPTER TWO                                24
    Sri Lanka's Colonial Past

CHAPTER THREE                              36
    Independence and Civil War

CHAPTER FOUR                               50
    The People of Sri Lanka

CHAPTER FIVE                               64
    Sri Lankan Arts and Culture

CHAPTER SIX                                78
    Sri Lanka at a Crossroads

    Facts About Sri Lanka                  90
    Notes                                  92
    Chronology                             95
    For Further Reading                   100
    Works Consulted                       102
    Index                                 107
    Picture Credits                       111
    About the Author                      112

# INTRODUCTION

## FALL FROM PARADISE

Sri Lanka, once called Ceylon, has long been praised by explorers and visitors for its incredible natural beauty and rich culture. Many have written about the island's environmental treasures and romantic charm. For example, writing in the 1960s, Sir Charles Jeffries, a high-ranking member of Britain's Colonial Office, describes the island he knew and loved as:

> A lovely land, a holy land. A land of ancient romance and modern bustle. A land where the age-old pattern of village life goes softly on its way alongside the seething energy of a great metropolis and trading centre. A land of fantastic colour and sound when the great processions of elephants go forth . . . and of quiet serenity when hill and forest sleep beneath the tropical moon.[1]

Early in its history, the island of Sri Lanka was, indeed, a beautiful and tranquil paradise.

## SRI LANKA'S CIVIL WAR

Since the 1980s, however, Sri Lanka has been troubled by violence and death. A bitter civil war between its majority ethnic group, the Sinhalese, and the minority Tamils has claimed many lives and destroyed much property. Actually, both groups have lived on the island for many centuries, and each can claim it is their beloved ancestral home. The two groups even lived together peaceably for many years and worked side by side to achieve Sri Lanka's independence from British colonialism in 1948. After independence, however, competition for power and prosperity created deep rifts that have only widened in ensuing years.

The first turning point in Sinhalese-Tamil relations came in 1948 and 1949 with the citizenship acts—legislation enacted by the new country to take away voting rights from Tamil immigrants who had been brought to the island to

Sri Lanka has long enjoyed a reputation among travelers as an island paradise. Pictured here is the beautiful seashore of the southern town of Galle.

work on its tea and rubber plantations during the colonial period. The action helped to ensure that the Tamils, who had gained favor with British colonists, would not be able to challenge Sinhalese majority rule. An even larger controversy surrounded the Official Language Act of 1956. This legislation designated the Sinhala language as the official language of the country instead of English. This decision further alienated the Tamils, who wanted their native language to be accorded equal status.

Yet a third turning point came with the election of S.W.R.D. Bandaranaike as prime minister in 1956. Bandaranaike's government ushered in an era of government action aimed mostly at promoting a Sinhalese and Buddhism-oriented nationalism based on the idea that only the Sinhalese embodied authentic Ceylonese culture. The Hindu Tamils, on the other hand, were regarded as a threat to Sinhalese nationhood and they were discriminated against by the government in crucial areas such as education and employment.

In the 1970s, when a new Sri Lankan government led by J.R. Jayewardene began trying to remedy the damage that had been done through years of anti-Tamil policies, it appeared to be too late for national unity. By then the Tamils had decided they wanted to break away from the Sinhalese to form an independent state in the northeastern part of the island. A group of radical Tamils had even formed a separatist group known as the Liberation Tigers of Tamil Eelam (LTTE) that advocated armed struggle to achieve Tamil independence from the rest of Sri Lanka. When the LTTE initiated terrorist attacks on government and other targets, the government responded with force and the civil war began in earnest.

## PROSPECTS FOR PEACE

In the two decades since the war began, the fighting between government soldiers and LTTE rebels has killed as many as sixty-four thousand Sri Lankans, many of them Tamil civilians caught in the middle of the fighting. It also has displaced tens of thousands more Tamils from their homes and farms. Large numbers of Tamils have simply given up on Sri Lanka and moved to southern India, but many still live in other parts of the island waiting for peace, when they hope to return to their ancestral lands. In the meantime, the civil war has literally divided the country in half, with the Sinhalese concentrated in the southern and eastern parts of the island and the Tamils segregated in the northeast.

Indeed, the fighting became so intense that in 1987 India intervened to negotiate a peace agreement and cease-fire, and then brought in Indian peace-keeping troops to maintain order. This effort, too, failed in the face of violence staged both by LTTE and an extremist Sinhalese group known as the People's Liberation Front (Janatha Vimukthi Peramuna, or JVP). India gave up and recalled its peace-keeping force in 1990.

Following the Indian withdrawal, Sri Lankans elected President Chandrika Kumaratunga, who promised to end the country's civil war. With the help of outside mediators, the government in 2002 negotiated a cease-fire that, although fragile, still holds today. Peace talks between LTTE and the government, however, broke down in 2003 and have yet to be resumed. In the absence of a true and lasting peace agreement, the country limps along economically and its people suffer, both psychologically and physically.

*A woman who lost two children in the devastating tsunami of December 2004 turns away from the ruins of her home in northern Sri Lanka.*

## THE 2004 TSUNAMI

More death and misery recently came to Sri Lanka in the form of a massive tsunami, which struck the island on December 26, 2004, as a result of a powerful undersea earthquake that occurred off the coast of the island of Sumatra, part of Indonesia. The monster waves created by the earthquake traveled north, hitting Sri Lanka's shorelines and flooding more than a mile inland. Along the way, the waves wiped out whole communities, washing away roads, telephone and electrical lines, houses, hotels, and hospitals.

People, too, were engulfed by the water, and many simply disappeared into the deep of the sea. Others were killed and found lying on the devastated beaches when the water retreated. Those lucky enough to survive were often left injured, orphaned, or missing other members of their family. Survivors also had no freshwater or food, no clothing or blankets to stay warm, and no shelter. Many countries in the region were struck just as hard, but the final body count in Sri Lanka was more than forty thousand dead or missing—almost as many people as were killed in twenty years of civil war—and more than a million were left homeless.

Although it was an unparalleled tragedy, many hope that the tsunami might mark a new beginning for Sri Lanka. By destroying roads and communications, the tsunami made it almost impossible to wage war, and the aftermath forced the country's two warring sides to at least talk about how to assist victims and structure recovery efforts. The disaster also is expected to bring in massive amounts of foreign aid, which experts say will give a much-needed boost to the country's economy. If Sri Lanka's leaders can act with vision to take advantage of this window of opportunity, perhaps the one-time paradise known as Sri Lanka can yet be saved.

# An Island Jewel

Sri Lanka is a tiny, tear-shaped jewel of an island that lies in the Indian Ocean, just south of India in South Asia. The island is only about 217 miles (349km) long and 112 miles (180km) wide at its widest part. The entire territory of the country, in fact, is only 25,332 square miles (65,610 sq.km), or about the size of the U.S. state of West Virginia. For such a small island, however, Sri Lanka is one of the most beautiful and scenic places on earth. As the travel Web site Lonely Planet notes, "Sri Lanka has many nicknames: Serendib, Ceylon, Teardrop of India, Resplendent Isle, Island of Dharma, Pearl of the Orient. This colorful collection [of names] reveals its richness and beauty, and the intensity of the affection it evokes in its visitors."[2]

## THREE GEOGRAPHIC ZONES

The island's beauty is created, in part, by a highly varied landscape that is marked by three main geographic zones—the central highlands, the plains, and the coastal belt. Towering mountains in the south-central part of Sri Lanka make up the heart of the island. This area, called the central highlands, contains some of the country's tallest peaks, which are separated by deep valleys and gorges. Pidurutalagala, a mountain located in the middle of the highlands area, is the highest peak and soars a remarkable 8,281 feet (2,524m) into the sky. Other very scenic mountains lie further to the south, including Namunakuli to the east at 6,680 feet (2,036m), and Sri Lanka's most famous mountain, Adam's Peak, to the west at 7,297 feet (2,224m). Although it is only the second-highest point in Sri Lanka's mountains, Adam's Peak (or Sri Pada) rises up in a giant conical shape that appears to be separated from surrounding mountains—a sight so unique and imposing that it has become the most well-known feature of the country's mountain landscape. As a Web site dedicated to Adam's Peak relates, "[The mountain's] position in relation to the [surrounding] topography is so dominant that it stands out above all others."[3]

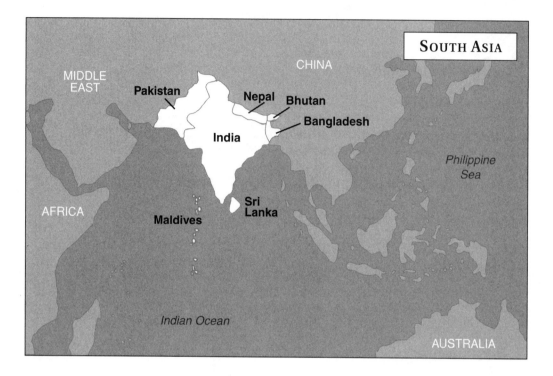

From these mountains, the land descends into a series of plains that make up the majority of the island's surface. In the southwestern part of the country, the land rises gradually toward the mountains, creating plains that are characterized by beautiful rolling hills. Here centuries of erosion have created rich soils for agriculture, and Sri Lankans historically have grown crops such as tea, rubber, and coconut. Sri Lanka is especially known for its fine teas, which grow throughout the southeast region. The southeastern plains, on the other hand, are flatter, and the land abruptly rises up like a wall toward the mountains. In the northern part of the island is an arid and relatively flat plain known as the dry zone. It is broken by long, narrow ridges of granite that stretch northward from the mountains.

Surrounding the island at about 100 feet (30.5m) above sea level is a coastal zone that consists mostly of spectacular sandy beaches intersected by numerous lagoons. However, at the northern tip of the island is a projection of land called the Jaffna Peninsula, where the beaches give way to low-lying limestone cliffs. South of Jaffna Peninsula on the northwest side of Sri Lanka lies Mannar Island, a tiny island that is joined to the Indian mainland by a chain of reefs, sandbanks, and islets called Adam's Bridge. A number of smaller islands also can be found off both the northeast and southwest shores. Sri Lanka's shores, too, are dotted with rocky cliffs and bays. These conditions have helped to create two of the world's best harbors—a large harbor at Trincomalee on the northeast coast and a smaller one at Galle in the southwestern part of the island. Indeed, the excellent harbor at Trincomalee has had great strategic value over the centuries, and various European powers—the Portuguese, the Dutch, the French, and the British—sought to control it.

### RIVERS AND WATERFALLS

In addition to its bays and harbors, Sri Lanka possesses many rivers, most of which begin in the mountains of the central highlands and flow through the gorges and valleys into the

## THE FOOTPRINT AT ADAM'S PEAK

Adam's Peak, one of Sri Lanka's tallest mountains, is considered sacred by Sri Lankans and has been a place of religious pilgrimage for more than a thousand years. Even today, during the months from December to April, pilgrims from many different religions climb Adam's Peak. At the top, they can view an indentation in the rock that is said to be an ancient footprint. Muslims claim the footprint was made by Adam, after he sinned in the Garden of Eden. Buddhists, on the other hand, believe it to be the mark of Buddha during his final visit to the island, and Hindus say the footprint was left by the Hindu god Shiva. Even Christians visit the peak, believing the footprint belongs to Saint Thomas, the apostle who first brought Christianity to Sri Lanka. British civil servant Sir Charles Jeffries, in his 1963 book, *Ceylon: The Path to Independence*, quotes historian Harry Williams as stating, Adam's Peak is "the most sacred mountain in the world, holy to one thousand million people."

*Pilgrims make their way down Adam's Peak, one of the most sacred places in Sri Lanka.*

plains before finally reaching the Indian Ocean. Although most of the country's rivers are quite short, a few travel for more than a hundred miles. The longest river is the Mahaweli, which winds northeasterly from a point south of the city of Kandy until it empties into the sea near Trincomalee—a distance of about 208 miles (335km). Sri Lanka's second-longest river, the Aruvi Aru, flows northwest for about 135 miles (217km) across the dry zone to a point near Mannar on the western coast. Still other important rivers include the Kelani, which flows into the ocean on the southwestern coast near the city of Colombo, and the Kalu, which reaches the sea south of Colombo. Adam's Peak is the main watershed area for Sri Lanka's river system. Four of the island's sixteen principal rivers, including the Mahaweli, originate here and then flow to the sea in many different directions.

Once in the plains, the rivers run slowly and often flood during rainy seasons. In the highlands, however, the rivers are typically wild and fast moving as they negotiate the rugged mountain terrain. This terrain creates spectacular waterfalls, some of which plunge from heights of more than 800 feet (244m). Of the country's more than one hundred waterfalls, the tallest is Bambarakande Falls, which during the wet season falls in a thick stream about 863 feet (263m) over a craggy rock wall. One of the island's most famous waterfalls, however, is Diyaluma Falls, which cascades like a misty veil about 722 feet (220m) into a large, deep pool. According to legend, a beautiful princess once fled to the waterfall with her commoner lover. There they pledged their eternal love and jumped to their deaths rather than be separated by their families.

Sri Lanka's rivers provide water for irrigation and drinking, particularly in the dryer northeast region. Indeed, as far back as two thousand years ago, the people of Sri Lanka built reservoirs, canals, and irrigation systems in the northern highlands to water their crops. Today the island's rivers and reservoirs have also been harnessed to produce hydroelectric power, the main source of energy for the country. In addition, the rivers over the centuries have washed a rich collection of gemstones from the highlands into the lowland valleys. For many centuries, Sri Lanka has been a source of rubies, sapphires, and semiprecious stones such as amethyst, alexandrite, and topaz.

## MILES OF BEACHES

Perhaps Sri Lanka's most prized geographical resource, however, is its coastlines and more than 620 miles (998km) of sandy, white beaches. Indeed, there are popular tourist beaches on all sides of the island, some with developed beach resorts. As one travel Web site notes, "Sri Lanka is never out of season for a beach holiday. There is always some part of the beach that has friendly and warm waters."[4]

Some of the most beautiful of Sri Lanka's beaches are located on Sri Lanka's northeastern coast, near the city of Trincomalee. Here the country is blessed with long stretches of warm beaches, many of which are good for fishing, snorkeling, and scuba diving. In addition, the western side of the city is surrounded by great expanses of scenic hill country that are protected by national parks. Sri Lanka's civil strife, however, has greatly affected this area and has deterred most visitors. As a result, tourism has barely touched the area, leaving it largely undeveloped and unseen by outsiders.

Instead the most popular beach areas today are located mostly in the southern part of the island. During the tourist season from October through April, tourists pour into this region looking for sun, sand, and relaxation. One very popular southern beach town, for example, is Hikkaduwa, located south of Colombo near Galle. The first Sri Lankan area to be

*Sri Lanka is very rich in marine resources. Here, fishermen perch on stilts on the beach at Kabalana as they fish for sardines.*

# SRI LANKA'S ELEPHANTS

Sri Lanka is one of the few places in the world where elephants can still be found in the wild. At the turn of the twentieth century, as many as 10,000 elephants roamed all over the island, but big-game hunting and deforestation have greatly reduced those numbers. Today, although estimates vary, as many as 2,500 to 3,000 elephants live in the country's forests and grasslands, mostly in the northeastern and eastern areas. Another 500 are confined to Sri Lanka's national parks. The Asian elephant found in Sri Lanka is similar to the African elephant, but with smaller ears, a slightly different shape, and more hair. Sri Lanka's wild elephants live in herds in which they are intimately connected to each other and form deep social bonds. Experts even believe that the herd celebrates when a member becomes pregnant and then gives the expectant mother extra attention. When the baby elephant is born after twenty-two months of gestation, all members of the herd touch the infant, running their trunks over its entire body and imprinting the baby as a new part of the herd.

*A wild Asian elephant calf takes food from its mother's mouth at Minneriya National Park in central Sri Lanka.*

developed for tourism, Hikkaduwa has numerous restaurants and cafés, and wide sandy beaches. It is most famous, however, for its marine sanctuary, which is abundant with rare corals and tropical fish. The reef lies just below the water and can be easily viewed by snorklers. The area around Hikkaduwa also has long been a favorite scuba diving and surfing spot. Unfortunately, Hiddakuwa was severely damaged by the 2004 tsunami and is only slowly being rebuilt.

In addition to Hikkaduwa, other parts of Sri Lanka's coast contain extensive coral reef habitats. Most of these are located in the northwestern and eastern coastal areas. There are also reefs around some of the islands near the Jaffna Peninsula. Altogether, a total of 183 species of stony corals have been recorded in Sri Lanka. These corals create a habitat for almost four hundred species of marine life, including a number of diverse butterfly fish species; invertebrates such as lobsters, shrimps, and crabs; and marine flora such as sea grasses and algae. Dolphins, whale sharks, and sea turtles can also be seen swimming in the island's reef systems. Many of Sri Lanka's reefs, however, have been severely damaged by human activities. The major causes of coral reef damage, for example, are coral mining and harvesting, destructive fishing activities, and damage caused by fishermen's boat anchors.

## FORESTS AND BIODIVERSITY

In addition to marine life, Sri Lanka teems with exotic plant and animal life. Forests once covered almost the entire island, but many were cleared for agriculture and development. Between 1796 and 1948, for example, the British removed close to half of the island's forests to make way for plantation crops such as tea, coffee, and rubber. Following independence, more trees were cleared due to industrialization and population growth.

Today dense evergreen rainforests are concentrated in the wet southwestern lowlands region. Here, in a pristine 22,000-acre (8,900ha) reserve known as the Sinharaja Forest, approximately 211 species of trees still grow, including many types of giant canopy trees that soar as high as 150 feet (46m). Underneath these trees is a dense undergrowth of vines and many different kinds of orchids. At higher elevations in the south and central parts of the island, subtropical evergreen forests, with broad-leaved trees similar to those found in temperate climates, thrive.

In the drier parts of the country, such as the southeast, east, and northern regions, the vegetation has adapted to conserve water. These areas feature hardy grasslands and shrubs, thorny trees such as flowering acacias, as well as more valuable tree species such as ebony, satinwood, ironwood, and mahogany. Along the coasts, pines and palm trees are the main tree species, and forests of mangrove, a type of tree adapted to water-logged soil, grow around the lagoons and river estuaries.

Sri Lanka's forested areas provide a home for thousands of animals, including 84 species of mammals, 435 recorded species of birds, 242 known species of butterflies, 107 species of fish, and over 400 species of amphibians, reptiles, and snakes. Some of the most well-known animals in Sri Lanka are elephants, leopards, monkeys, crocodiles, sloth bears, bears, jackals, wild boar, snakes such as cobras and pythons, peacocks, and flying foxes, batlike mammals that live in tree-top colonies. The island also is known for its exotic birds. Many of these are migrating birds, including parrots and flamingos, which travel south to the island's lagoons and wetlands to escape the northern winters.

Indeed, despite its tiny size, Sri Lanka has a truly remarkable amount of biodiversity. As reporter Charlie Furniss explains, "It has a proportionally high number of endemic [native] species: 23 per cent of its 3,400 flowering plants, 16 per cent of its 84 mammals and 43 per cent of its 162 reptiles are found nowhere else in the world."[5] The island is even home to more than 250 species of frogs, which account for 7 percent of the world's known frog species.

To help protect the environment, the government has set aside several nature sanctuaries. In fact, 13 percent of Sri Lanka's land area has been designated for wildlife and nature conservation. Despite these efforts, however, deforestation and environmental damage have clearly left their mark on the island. In 1991 a study based on satellite pictures concluded that only 22 percent of the country was still forested. Today the threat to Sri Lanka's forests continues as villages and plantations expand and trees are cut for timber. Sri Lanka's forests also have been recently damaged by the country's civil war. Rebels often seek refuge in the forests, so

*Macaques are just one of the eighty-four species of mammals that make their home in the forested areas of Sri Lanka.*

the government has routinely cleared forests as a way to control the fighting. In addition, many people who have become displaced from their homes by war have moved into forested areas seeking new land. Forests, too, are cut as a source of fuel; many Sri Lankans still use firewood for cooking. The reduction of forest habitats has also caused some of the country's animals to be similarly endangered. Twenty-two species of mammals, for example, are now threatened with extinction.

## SETTLEMENTS AND POPULATION

Since ancient times, Sri Lanka's forested lands have been developed for agriculture, and its coastlines have attracted fishing communities. Today many small fishing villages remain, particularly on the less-developed eastern side of the island, and rice-growing villages still dot the interior landscape, along with irrigated fields containing other longtime money

*The capital city of Colombo on the southwestern coast is a bustling metropolis.*

crops such as tea, rubber, and coconut trees. Early fishing settlements on the southwestern coast were eventually linked by a coastal highway and railway. Over the years, these villages grew to include larger cities and urban centers. Much of Sri Lanka's population is now centered in these coastal urban centers.

One of the country's main urban areas, for example, is Colombo, a seaport on the southwestern coast. Colombo is Sri Lanka's largest city, with a population of about 1.5 million, and the nation's capital. The administrative capital of Sri Lanka is actually a suburb of Colombo, a town called Sri Jayawardenepura (formerly Kotte). Colombo is also the country's commercial and business center, and a busy port. As one travel Web site describes it, the city is "noisy, frenetic—and just a little crazy,"[6] with constant traffic snarls and periodic power outages. Yet it is an interesting blend of old and new. Charming old colonial buildings, a seafront park used for cricket games, and numerous Buddhist and Hindu temples coexist with many new shopping malls and modern businesses. In addition, the city is the site of the National Museum, containing historical items; an art gallery that features local artists; and the Dehiwala Zoo, a great place to see Sri Lankan elephants.

A second major southern city is the seaport of Galle. It is located on the southwestern coast south of Colombo. Galle is a major agricultural marketing and shipping center, where goods such as tea, rubber, coconut oil, cloves, and other products from the island's interior are shipped for distribution around the world. Galle is also known for its old Dutch fort that was built in 1663. The walls of this imposing structure still protect a number of Dutch houses, museums, and churches. Unfortunately, Galle was one of the cities damaged by the 2004 tsunami, and many of its buildings are in need of repair.

Another important Sri Lankan city is Kandy, the so-called capital of the hill country. Kandy is located in the central highlands region and has a population of about 108,000. It once was the capital of the Sinhalese kingdom of Kandy, until it was annexed by the British in 1815. Today it is the market center for surrounding tea, rubber, rice, and cacao farms. Built around a peaceful and scenic artificial lake, the city of Kandy is also a mountain resort with great architectural character and a collection of old shops, buses, markets, and

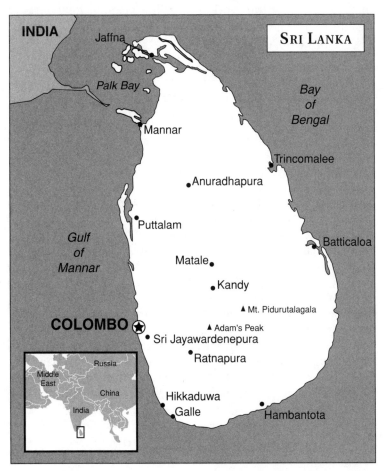

hotels. The city's most famous attraction is the Dalada Mali-gawa (or Temple of the Tooth), a temple that contains Sri Lanka's most important religious relic—the sacred tooth of Buddha. The relic has made Kandy a tourist attraction, and it is honored with an annual pageant. Kandy is also known as the site of the University of Sri Lanka and famous botanical gardens that are noted for their orchids.

Sri Lanka's Tamil population, however, is concentrated in two main northern urban areas—the northwestern seaport of Jaffna, located on the Jaffna Peninsula, and Trincomalee, a seaport on the northeastern coast. Jaffna is the center of the Tamil heartland and has been the site of many battles be-tween Tamil rebels and government forces. It was once Sri Lanka's second-largest city until the country's civil war drove away much of its population. Trincomalee, with its beautiful harbor and great tourist potential, has also has been largely isolated from the rest of the country by the civil war and lack of economic development.

 **FEAR OF A SECOND TSUNAMI**

Following the December 26, 2004, tsunami disaster, traumatized Sri Lankans and people throughout Southeast Asia had a new respect for nature's fury and lived in fear of another earthquake. These fears were realized three months later on March 28, 2005, when a second powerful earthquake struck just 200 miles (322km) south of the site of the December earthquake, off the coast of Sumatra, Indone-sia. The earthquake had a magnitude of 8.7 and sent Sri Lanka's frightened residents scurrying toward the hills in fear of a second tsunami. Sri Lankan officials alerted the media; and the police, the military, and even Buddhist monasteries used loudspeakers to wake up and warn coastal residents to get away from the coastlines. As sixty-four-year-old Sri Lankan grandmother M. Chandralatha explained to reporter Alisa Tang of the Associated Press in a March 29, 2005 article, "One of our neighbors knocked at our door and told us the tsunami was coming, so we ran." This time, however, the people of Sri Lanka were spared, because the earthquake did not generate tsunami waves. But one area was severely damaged by the new quake—the small Indonesian island of Nias, where one thousand to two thousand people were feared dead.

## CLIMATE AND THE 2004 TSUNAMI

The island owes much of its natural variety and agricultural riches to its tropical climate, which provides both warmth and moisture. Average temperatures range from about 60°F (16°C) in the central highlands to 85°F (29°C) on the northeast coast. However, temperatures at times can reach freezing in the mountains and close to 100°F (38°C) along the warmer coastal lowlands. November through January is the coolest period, while February through May is the hottest.

The most important climate pattern on the island is the monsoon winds that blow from the Indian Ocean during two distinct seasons. In early June through October, known as Yala season, winds from the southwest bring heavy rain to the southern and western coasts, and the central highlands. Incredibly, some areas of the island during this period receive as much as 97 inches (246.4cm) of rain per month. During the December through March period, known as Maha season, winds blow from the opposite, northeastern side of the island, bringing substantial, although less, rain to the northeast side of the island. These areas can get up to 50 inches (127cm) of rain each month. The monsoon storms occasionally even grow to highly dangerous cyclone or tornado proportions. In 1964, for example, both India and Sri Lanka (then Ceylon) were hit by a cyclone and 4,850 people were killed.

Besides these monsoons, Sri Lanka is usually not subject to other destructive natural forces such as earthquakes or volcanic eruptions. On December 26, 2004, however, the country did not escape when a magnitude 8.9 undersea earthquake off the coast of nearby Indonesia caused a massive tsunami that brought walls of water onto the eastern and southern coasts of the island, killing and injuring tens of thousands and leaving more than a million people homeless. On this day, Sri Lanka's sunny, tropical beauty was marred by so much death and destruction that even the country's warring factions put down their arms to rush to the aid of the tsunami's victims.

# 2

# SRI LANKA'S COLONIAL PAST

Sri Lanka was first settled thousands of years ago by two ethnic groups from India—the Sinhalese and the Tamils. Throughout its more recent history, however, Sri Lanka was ruled by several different European colonial powers, each of which explored the island for its trade and agricultural riches. The island did not achieve full independence until 1948.

## ANCIENT SETTLEMENTS AND KINGDOMS

Sri Lanka's history dates back more than two thousand years. One of the earliest references to the island is in the Indian epic called *Ramayana*, which is believed to have been written around 500 B.C. by a Hindu god. The most important early record of the island's history, however, is contained in Buddhist chronicles—the *Mahavamsa* and its sequel, *Culavamsa*—written by monks in the sixth century A.D. The *Mahavamsa* and the *Culavamsa* record the rise and fall of early Buddhist kingdoms beginning with Vijaya, an Indian prince who is believed to be the ancestor of the Sinhalese, Sri Lanka's majority ethnic group.

The epic *Mahavamsa* says that Vijaya arrived on the island around the fifth century B.C. with a group of about seven hundred settlers from the coastal areas of northern India. Vijaya was the son of an Indian king, Sinha (meaning the Lion), who gave the Sinhalese people their name. According to the legend, Vijaya became the ruler of the first kingdom on the island, and his descendants established successive Sinhalese kingdoms. The capital of this Sinhalese territory was Anuradhapura, a powerful city-state founded by King Pandukabhaya in 437 B.C. about 128 miles (206km) north of the modern city of Colombo on the banks of the Malwatu Oya river. Anuradhapura remained the royal seat of more than 250 Buddhist and Hindu kings for the next 1,400 years. During this period, the Sinhalese conquered the land and jungles throughout the island and built extensive reservoirs and canals to grow rice and other crops. Anuradhapura also became a center for advanced learning, art, and culture.

Buddhism was first introduced to the island in the third century B.C. by the mighty Indian emperor King Aśoka who sought to spread Buddhism throughout the region. Aśoka was such a true believer in Buddhism that he sent his own son, Mahinda, to meet with Sinhalese king Devanampiya Tissa and introduce him to the religion. Mahinda's sermons were warmly embraced by the king, and Buddhism quickly became accepted by both the royal classes and ordinary people. King Devanampiya Tissa even made Buddhism the official religion of his kingdom. The king also built numerous monasteries and constructed the Thuparama Dagoba, the first stupa (or Buddhist shrine) in Anuradhapura, to house some of the Buddha's relics, such as pieces of his bones. Within fifty years, Buddhism had spread throughout the island and was firmly established. The influence of the new religion helped the Sinhalese people to work together in peace and harmony to build a prosperous and literate society that lasted for many centuries.

Over time, however, the power of the Sinhalese kings declined and the Sinhalese kingdoms were invaded by a people from southern India called the Tamils, who spoke the Dravidian language and followed the Hindu religion. The Tamils did not mix with the Sinhalese but instead kept to themselves and retained their own religion, language, and culture. They settled mostly in the northern part of the island and eventually challenged the

*This picture shows a stone relief of Buddha in Anuradhapura, the birthplace of Sinhalese civilization.*

Sinhalese rule there. The Tamil threat began as early as 237 B.C., when Tamil adventurers Sena and Guttika took control of Anuradhapura for twenty-two years. Later, in 145 B.C., a Tamil general named Elara rose to the throne at Anuradhapura and ruled for forty-four years. In succeeding centuries, the Tamil threat to the Sinhalese became even more real as three separate Hindu empires from southern India—the Pandya, Pallava, and Cōla—all sought to control Sri Lanka.

Finally, in the tenth century, the Cōla empire destroyed Anuradhapura and moved the capital to Polonnaruwa, an easily defensible site just north of the modern city of Kandy. The Sinhalese fought back, however, and later reestablished control of northern Sri Lanka, with Polonnaruwa as their new capital. As social scientist Peter R. Blood notes, during the reign of the great Sinhalese king Parakramabahu I, who ruled from A.D. 1153 to 1186 the new city of Polonnaruwa even "grew to rival Anuradhapura in architectural diversity and as a repository of Buddhist art."[7]

However, the pressure of the repeated Tamil invasions, together with other factors such as a breakdown in the Sinhalese social order and a large-scale outbreak of malaria, eventually caused the Sinhalese to withdraw from the northern dry zones. By the thirteenth century A.D., the Tamil Hindus largely controlled the northern part of the island, forcing the Sinhalese into the southern and central regions. Separated by dense jungle and interior mountains, the two peoples thereafter developed completely separate cultures. With the exception of a brief period during the reign of King Parakramabahu VI in A.D. 1412–1467, the Sinhalese never again ruled the entire island.

## PORTUGUESE SETTLERS

Europeans first arrived in Sri Lanka in the sixteenth century. In 1505 Portuguese explorer Lourenço de Almeida discovered the island by accident when a storm forced his ship to land at Galle on the island's western coast. At this time, Sri Lanka was ruled by a northern Tamil kingdom based in Jaffna and two southern Sinhalese kingdoms—Kotte and Kandy. The Portuguese were met by a friendly King Parakramabahu VIII, the king of Kotte, who offered the visitors gifts of cinnamon and elephants. With the king's permis-

# THE GLORY OF ANURADHAPURA

Situated 128 miles (206km) north of Colombo on the banks of the Malwatu Oya river, the ancient city of Anuradhapura was the capital of the Sinhalese kingdom on the island of Sri Lanka for over fourteen hundred years. During its heyday, Anuradhapura was not only a center of Sinhalese political power but also a preeminent site of wealth and culture, and a sacred place for Buddhists. The city had three-story houses and thriving businesses, as well as a bejewelled palace and many gold shrines.

Anuradhapura today is one of the world's major archaeological sites. Although many wood structures have not survived, several magnificent temples, palaces, bathing ponds, monasteries, hospitals, and other structures still stand, attesting to the city's glorious past. Some of the most important ruins are three huge *dagobas* [or stupas]—domed shrines containing sacred relics or bodily remains of the Buddha-called Ruvanveli, Jetavana, and Abhayagiri. Another historical item at Anuradhapura is the sacred bo tree (Sri Maha Bodhi), which is said to be grown from a branch of the very tree under which the Buddha attained enlightenment in India. Throughout the ruins of the city are magnificent, ancient Buddha images and stone sculptures.

*Ruwanweli Dagoba, a Buddhist temple in Anuradhapura, houses some of Sri Lanka's most important shrines.*

sion, Portugal also quickly established a trading base at Colombo.

The Portuguese soon revealed that they intended to use the island as a strategic base to protect and increase Portugal's share of the Indian Ocean spice trade. Spices such as cinnamon, nutmeg, and cloves, which only grew in this part of the world, were highly popular in Europe at this time and brought high prices and great profits. The Portuguese therefore sought to extend their power over the island, which they called Cilao. Over the next century, through military might and political maneuvering, they managed to gain control over the northern Tamil kingdom of Jaffna as well as the southern Sinhalese kingdom of Kotte. In the Portuguese parts of the island, the Portuguese ruled as colonizers, forcing indigenous peoples to provide free labor and to convert from Buddhism to Roman Catholicism, the Christian religion of Portugal. As Jeffries explains, "The record of the sixteenth century [on the island] is one of almost unrelieved misery."[8]

However, the Portuguese were never able to subdue the powerful Kandy Sinhalese kingdom. Although the Portuguese tried to install a leader on the Kandy throne who would be loyal to them, this effort failed. Instead the Kandyans fought the Europeans fiercely each time soldiers were sent into the kingdom. Eventually, the king of Kandy agreed to negotiations with another European power, the Dutch, for help against the Portuguese.

## THE DUTCH INVASION

The Dutch, like the Portuguese, were attracted to Sri Lanka because of its spices and its strategic position on the spice trading routes. By the end of the sixteenth century, the Dutch had already established a trading post in nearby Java (an island that today is part of Indonesia) as part of a strategy to

*In the seventeenth century, the Dutch came to Sri Lanka in order to monopolize the island's spice trade. The fort in Galle stands as a reminder of the Dutch colonial period.*

capture the Indian spice trade from Portugal. In 1612 Dutch traders contacted the king of Kandy and agreed to help Kandy fight the Portuguese in exchange for a monopoly on part of the island's trade goods, primarily cinnamon. Thereafter, the Dutch captured parts of the island such as the eastern port of Trincomalee from the Portuguese and returned them to Kandy. Later Dutch victories against the Portuguese, however, did not result in the restoration of Sinhalese rule over the entire island because the Dutch decided to keep control of the island's spice-growing areas. By 1646 the Dutch occupied all of the cinnamon-producing regions, and the king of Kandy realized that he had simply replaced one master with another.

Within a few years, the Dutch had established control over most of the Portuguese parts of the island. After extensive fighting, the Portuguese abandoned Colombo in 1656 and surrendered their last stronghold at Jaffna two years later. The Dutch, however, unlike the Portuguese, were concerned less with conquest and interested more in controlling the island's trade. They therefore allowed the Sinhalese Kandy kingdom to remain intact in the central and eastern regions, and occupied only the lowlands of the island. For the next century, the two powers coexisted in this manner as the Dutch focused on monopolizing trade on the island. The Dutch did so through the Dutch East India Company, a powerful entity created by the Dutch government to carry out and protect trading activities in Southeast Asia.

To promote peaceful and effective trade relations, the Dutch made many improvements during their stay in Sri Lanka, which they called Ceylon. Given the chaotic state of the island produced by wars with the Portuguese, one of the first such improvements was the establishment of law and order through a Dutch-Roman judicial and government system. Under this system, Dutch governors were appointed to govern three main provinces, but local customs, laws, and institutions were left largely intact. The Dutch also built roads and bridges, provided some limited education and social services, introduced new crops and industries, and in general began to develop the island's economy. These improvements helped to raise the standard of living for many indigenous people living in Dutch-controlled areas. The Sinhalese who continued to live in the Kandy kingdom, meanwhile, declined somewhat in prosperity but nevertheless were proud that they remained independent of European rule.

## BRITISH RULE

Britain was the first European power to control the entire island. The British became interested in Sri Lanka in the mid-eighteenth century because they wanted an all-weather port in the region. After the Dutch refused to grant them permission to dock ships at Trincomalee, the British took the port by force in 1796 and then ousted the Dutch from the remainder of the island. Within a short time, the British were also able to undermine the king of Kandy and bring the Kandy areas under their control. By 1818 all of the island was officially under British rule and called the Crown Colony of Ceylon.

The Portuguese and the Dutch each had their impact on the island, but the British influence would prove to be the most important and lasting. During this last colonial period, for example, Britain completely changed the island's economy. The British built a network of roads and railways, opened schools and hospitals, and constructed modern communications systems and hydroelectric plants for energy. Most importantly, in the mid-1830s, the British established large agricultural plantations in the highlands to grow coffee, which became one of Britain's most successful colonial exports. The coffee plantations, however, required more laborers than could be found in the native population, so Britain imported cheap Tamil laborers from southern India to do the harvesting each year. After the harvests, the workers would return to their homes in India.

This British plantation system transformed the island's economy from subsistence agriculture into a viable agricultural export economy, changing the focus from growing crops for food to growing crops that could be exported for profit. As Blood explains, "The plantation system dominated the economy in Sri Lanka to such an extent that one observer described the government as an 'appendage of the [plantations].'"[9] The system made both British and some Sri Lankan landowners rich, but by emphasizing commercial crops over food, it also produced famines and poverty for many rural peasants.

In 1870, however, a disastrous leaf disease devastated the coffee industry, forcing planters to search for new crops. The main substitute that was found was Indian tea plants, which thrived in the highland conditions. Farmers also had some success with another crop, rubber trees. Tea and rubber, unlike coffee, were harvested throughout the year and required a permanent labor force. This encouraged the Indian Tamils and their families to settle on the plantations, where they formed a permanent, underpaid, and poorly housed Sri Lankan underclass. Thereafter, tea became the island's most important export for the next century. Even today, fine Ceylon tea is a key export product and is known around the world by tea connoisseurs.

Another part of the British legacy was a philosophy toward its colonies that called for them to be treated more as trusteeships entitled to certain economic, educational, and political freedoms. Under this approach, first proposed by the royal Colebrook-Cameron Commission in 1833, Britain

---

 ## CEYLON TEAS

Sri Lanka (then called Ceylon) began growing tea in the late 1800s, after a disease killed the majority of its coffee plants. Tea soon replaced coffee as the island's main agricultural crop and is still marketed under the name "Ceylon" tea. Most of the best tea plantations are located at high elevations between 3,000 and 8,000 feet (914 to 2,438m) in two areas of the southwestern part of the island—east of Colombo and near the city of Galle to the south. Tea also grows in lower elevations, but the quality is not as good. As late as 1971, the majority of Sri Lanka's tea estates were still owned and run by British companies. In 1971, however, Sri Lanka enacted a Land Reform Act that redistributed many of the tea lands to the government. Sri Lanka was once the world's number one producer of tea, but in recent years production has fallen off due to the

 country's political and economic problems. Also, Sri Lanka faces increasing competition because its teas, although considered some of the best in the world, are not suitable for use in teabags.

*Tea pickers bring bushels of their harvest to a factory in the province of Uva.*

pulled back from its tight colonial control and introduced a number of reforms on the island. Most importantly, these reforms, for the first time, united the island's many different ethnic groups into five provinces that were placed under one "Crown Colony" government and judicial system that covered the entire island. Under this system, an Executive Council of senior British officials was created to advise the British governor and a Legislative Council was given the power to pass laws that would affect the entire island. The Legislative Council included nine British officials and six unofficial members to be appointed by the governor. The first unofficial members were three British merchants and three Sri Lankan representatives selected from the Sinhalese, Tamils, and Burghers (a community of mixed European and Sri Lankan ancestry). The reforms also allowed Sri Lankans for the first time to become administrators in the island's civil service, to be educated in English schools, and to take up trades associated with the new plantation economy. English became the island's national language.

## THE SRI LANKAN NATIONALIST MOVEMENT

The British reform efforts in the mid–nineteenth century not only established a united country but they also helped to create an educated class of Sri Lankans that began calling for involvement in government affairs and eventually independence from British rule. As Jeffries explains,

> The expansion of the educational system and the general development of the country resulted in the creation of a growing middle class drawn from [both] the Sinhalese people and the Tamil community. The professions, commerce and industry came increasingly to be staffed by the people of the island, and although political power still rested with the British officials and colonists, the days of their social and economic domination were numbered.[10]

One of the first signs of Sri Lankan nationalism, or patriotism, was the Sinhalese community's renewed interest in Buddhism, which over the years of colonial rule had been persecuted by colonial powers who introduced their own Christian religions to Sri Lanka. Part of this resurgence of

Buddhism focused on study of the past Sinhala-Buddhist domination of the island. Three Buddhist colleges and numerous other schools were established to teach Buddhist thought and history, and archaeologists began working at Anuradhapura and Polonnaruwa to uncover knowledge about ancient Buddhist kingdoms. This new information and learning helped to stimulate Sinhalese national pride. It was not long before the educated Sinhalese, together with educated Tamils, began to demand a greater voice in government and public affairs.

In 1910, under pressure from nationalist reformers, Britain made a small concession—it permitted a small electorate of Sri Lankans to elect one "educated Ceylonese" to the Legislative Council. This marked the first time Sri Lankans had any say in who represented their interests in the colonial government. Prior to this time, the Sri Lankan representatives on the council had been appointed by Britain and simply charged with representing various local communities. Following World War I, Sri Lankans began to make even more demands for change. In 1915 riots even broke out because of Sri Lankan dissatisfaction with the British Crown government. Fearing a challenge to their rule, the British

*In this photo from the 1880s, elephants carry religious objects and worshipers in a Buddhist procession through the streets of Colombo.*

overreacted, putting down the uprising by military force and killing a number of innocent civilians. The British government also declared martial law and arrested several prominent Sri Lankan leaders.

The harsh British response in 1915 only served to galvanize Sri Lankan nationalists, inspiring even stronger demands for local representation in the colonial government. As one Web page on Sri Lanka's history explains, "This [event] was considered the turning point in the nationalist movement in Sri Lanka."[11] A growing movement seeking independence from British rule in neighboring India also helped to inspire Sri Lankan reform. As a result, in 1919 several major Sinhalese and Tamil political organizations

*Sri Lankans supported the British during WWII. In this photograph, Tamil laborers manually whirl the propeller of a British war plane in 1944.*

formed the Ceylon National Congress to press for government reforms.

The demands of the congress ultimately led to amendments to the island's constitution in 1924 that expanded the Legislative Council to include a majority of elected Sri Lankan members. These reforms made the island government more representative. Real power, however, was still in the hands of British authorities, because only a tiny percentage of Sri Lankans were allowed to vote for the Legislative Council members and no Sri Lankans were permitted on the Executive Council. When discontent with this system continued, the British in 1927 set up a commission, the Donoughmore Commission, to study possible self-rule for the island. The commission's work in 1931 produced more constitutional changes, this time granting suffrage (or the right to vote) to all adult Sri Lankans and setting up a new legislature (the State Council) made up only of Sri Lankans. The new government system, however, was still subservient to a British governor, and no critical decisions could be made without the approval of the British.

## Independence

The outbreak of the Second World War in 1939 did not stop the Sri Lankan nationalists from continuing to push for their right to govern themselves. It was Sri Lanka's wholehearted cooperation with Britain and the Allies during World War II, however, that helped to convince Britain to move toward full independence for the island. The first step in this direction was Britain's decision to discuss the island's political status with Don Stephen Senanayake, a prominent member of the State Council and the leader of a coalition of nationalist groups called the United National Party (UNP). These talks resulted in the Ceylon Independence Act of 1947, a British law that provided for an official and peaceful transfer of power from Britain to an independent local government.

That same year, elections were held and were easily won by the UNP. Under a British system of government in which the head of the government is the prime minister, UNP leader Senanayake became the new country's first prime minister. A new constitution went into effect on February 4, 1948, officially making Sri Lanka, still called Ceylon at the time, an independent country.

# 3

# INDEPENDENCE
# AND CIVIL WAR

Although Sri Lanka gained its independence from European colonialism in 1948, it almost immediately slid into a prolonged ethnic struggle that has culminated in recent decades in a violent civil war between the ruling Sinhalese majority and the minority Tamil population. The conflict has caused deep psychological wounds and has so far prevented the government from unifying its people into one nation. Only recently has there been some cause for hope.

## THE SEEDS OF ETHNIC CONFLICT

Although the Tamils and Sinhalese had worked together during the early nationalist movement, tensions arose over the years as the Sinhalese began to outnumber Tamils in the colonial legislature. After Sri Lanka achieved independence in 1948, the new country immediately faced ethnic issues. One of the most pressing of these was how to classify the Indian Tamil immigrants brought to the island by Britain to work on tea and rubber plantations during the colonial period.

At first, Prime Minister Senanayake's sensitivity to minority interests seemed to hold promise for a united country. Senanayake's UNP embraced all ethnicities, and the new constitution included protections for minorities Senanayake was even able to convince G.G. Ponnambalam, the most prominent Tamil leader and head of the Ceylon Tamil Congress, to join his cabinet. Still, the nation remained divided. The establishment of Indian Tamil enclaves in what had been the Sinhalese-populated central highlands increasingly led to conflicts between the two groups over land and employment opportunities. The majority Sinhalese were also concerned that the Indian plantation workers could add to the political strength of the minority Ceylon Tamils, who had lived on the island for centuries. These pressures caused Senanayake to support three pieces of citizenship legislation in 1948 and 1949 that ultimately deprived the Indian Tamils of citizenship and voting rights.

The Indian Tamil citizenship issue revealed the divisions between and within the country's Tamil and Sinhalese political groups. One consequence of the debate, for example, was that the major Tamil party at that time—the moderate Ceylon Tamil Congress—split in two. A faction led by S.J.V. Chelvanayakam broke away from the main party to create a rival Tamil Federal Party. The new party advocated a much more aggressive stance against the Sinhalese and eventually replaced the Ceylon Tamil Congress as the dominant Tamil leadership. This development marked a significant change in Tamil-Sinhalese relations and set the stage for more serious conflict between the two ethnic groups.

The disagreements over ethnicity caused growing political unrest in the new country. The instability was only heightened when Senanayake was killed in a horseback-riding accident in

## THE OFFICIAL LANGUAGE ACT

Sri Lanka's 1948 constitution specifically protected the rights of minorities. It stated: "No . . . law shall . . . make persons of any community or religion liable to disabilities or restrictions to which any persons of other communities or religions are not made liable; or . . . confer on persons or any community or religion any privilege or advantage which is not conferred on persons of other communities or religions." Despite this constitutional provision, Sri Lanka's government in 1956 adopted the Official Language Act, which provided: "The Sinhala language shall be the one official Language of Ceylon." The Tamils felt this was a discriminatory and unconstitutional provision adopted by the majority population, and one that put them at a distinct disadvantage. It placed the Tamil language in an inferior position and required the Tamils to learn Sinhalese. Thus the law made it much more difficult for Tamils to obtain jobs in the government, the major employer for those with administrative skills. Because of these effects, the act was one of the most significant early sparks that ignited the ethnic conflict between the Sinhalese and the Tamils.

1952 and was succeeded by his son Dudley Senanayake. The senior Senanayake was a leader who had been committed to uniting Sri Lanka and providing more rights to minorities; his loss shook the government. Sri Lanka's troubles increased even more as its population growth outpaced its production of goods, creating economic problems. The government responded by reducing its subsidy of rice, the staple food on the island, an action that caused violent protests and eventually forced Dudley Senanayake's resignation.

### THE SLFP GOVERNMENT AND THE LANGUAGE ACT

In the face of these ethnic and economic problems, the UNP was defeated in 1956 by a rival party—the Sri Lanka Freedom Party (SLFP) led by Solomon West Ridgeway Dias Bandaranaike. The 1956 election proved to be another major turning point for the country. The new government rejected the UNP's links with Western culture and adopted socialist policies marked by government takeovers of businesses and

*In 1956 Prime Minister Bandaranaike made Sinhala the official language of Sri Lanka, a move that alienated the island's Tamil population.*

banks, and the expansion of social welfare programs. In addition, the SLFP government abandoned Senanayake's vision of a multi-ethnic country and instead promoted a Sinhalese-based nationalism. This Sinhalese viewpoint traced authentic Ceylonese culture only through Buddhism and Sinhalese political history. The minority Tamils were seen as a threat to this idea of nationhood. Many Sinhalese believed that the Tamils had prospered through an unfair share of education and power during the colonial period at the expense of the Sinhalese majority. As Blood explains, "Bandaranaike campaigned as the 'defender of a besieged Sinhalese culture' and demanded radical changes in the system."[12]

The most important change enacted by the new government was the Official Language Act of 1956. This legislation designated the Sinhala language as the country's official language instead of English. Although motivated by a desire to remove foreign, colonial influences from the island, the language law made Sinhala the only official language instead of giving the Tamil language equal importance. The law therefore caused the Tamils to feel that their language and culture were of no consequence, creating an even deeper rift between the two ethnic groups.

The Tamils responded by pressuring the government to allow their people a measure of autonomy in the northern part of the island. An agreement was even reached on this issue between Tamil leader S.J.V. Chelvanayakam and Prime Minister Bandaranaike. The agreement, however, was ultimately abandoned in the wake of the nation's first major episode of ethnic violence. In May 1958, violent Sinhalese riots erupted across the nation due to a rumor that a Tamil had killed a Sinhalese. The riots left hundreds of Tamils dead, caused the government to relocate twenty-five thousand Tamils from Sinhalese areas, and left a deep wound in Sri Lanka's society.

Bandaranaike was assassinated in September 1959 by a Buddhist extremist, but his wife, Sirimavo Bandaranaike, won the 1960 elections, becoming the world's first female prime minister. In addition to carrying out SLFP socialist policies, Mrs. Bandaranaike firmly enforced the language act. When Tamils in the north protested, she declared a state of emergency and restricted their political activities. Her great zeal in enforcing the pro-Sinhala policies of her husband led to even worse Tamil-Sinhalese relations.

## THE UNITED FRONT AND THE TULF

Bandaranaike's party was defeated in the next elections, and the UNP ruled from 1965 to 1970. This period was still marked by continuing ethnic tensions. This time, ethnic hostilities revolved around the 1966 Tamil Language Regulations, enacted by the UNP as a concession to the Tamils. This legislation permitted the Tamil language to be used for certain official purposes in Tamil areas. Sinhalese activists vigorously protested the law, prompting the government to declare a year-long state of emergency. Economic problems also hounded the government and helped to ensure a quick UNP ouster.

The 1970 elections brought Mrs. Bandaranaike back as prime minister as part of a new coalition party called the United Front. The United Front attacked the UNP for its alliance with the Tamils and promised to restore Sinhalese Buddhism to prominence. Soon after achieving power, the new government fulfilled this promise. In 1972 the United Front adopted a new constitution that made Buddhism the country's primary religion. In addition, the constitution changed Ceylon's name to Sri Lanka and declared the country to be a republic, with the legislative, executive, and judicial branches of government all concentrated in the National State Assembly.

The new constitution alarmed many Sri Lankans who worried that the new concentration of power might lead to an authoritarian government. The Tamils were particularly concerned because the constitution deleted a provision contained in the 1948 constitution that had provided protections for minorities. Indeed, the new constitution led to even greater discrimination against the Tamils. Under the new constitution, for example, the government in 1973 implemented a policy that made university admissions criteria easier for Sinhalese than for Tamils. As history professor Alan J. Bullion explains, "The result was a further decrease in employment opportunities for Tamil youth, in a stagnant economic climate, which increased ethnic tension."[13]

The Tamils perceived these government actions as a continuing government assault on Tamil society. In response, two Tamil parties—the Ceylon Tamil Congress and the Tamil Federal Party—united in 1972 to found the Tamil United Front (later called the Tamil United Liberation Front, or

TULF). The group issued a six-point plan in 1972 that demanded regional self-rule for the Tamils. Specifically, the plan demanded (1) that the Tamil language be recognized as a national language alongside Sinhala; (2) that citizenship be granted to all Indian Tamils; (3) that Sri Lanka be declared a secular state in which all religions are equal; (4) that the constitution guarantee fundamental freedom and rights for all; (5) that certain discriminatory religious ideas be abolished; and (6) that a decentralized government be created as a basis for participatory democracy. By 1976, however, TULF took an even stronger stand and began advocating full independence for the Tamils. As a TULF manifesto from this period explained, TULF wanted to "establish an independent, secular, socialist state of Tamil Eelam."[14]

*As prime minister, Sirimavo Bandaranaike continued to enforce her husband's pro-Sinhalese policies.*

## UNP LEADER JAYEWARDENE AND TAMIL TERRORISM

The UNP returned to power in 1977 after winning elections by a landslide. Voters responded to the vision of the UNP's new leader, Junius Richard Jayewardene, a longtime UNP supporter who promoted the party as the force for the creation of a just, fair, and peaceful Sri Lankan society. The UNP promised to address problems confronting the Tamils, such as education and employment, and as prime minister, Jayewardene wanted to ease tensions between the Tamils and the Sinhalese.

Jayewardene's first step was to change the constitution to replace the parliamentary, British-style government with a new government system that gave the president more power. Under this new system, still in place today, the president is elected every six years by the whole country and is given complete executive power. The president then chooses a cabinet of ministers to help him govern. Local provinces also have their own assemblies and government. Jayewardene assumed office as Sri Lanka's first president in 1978 and was re-elected in 1982 for a second term.

Using these new powers, Jayewardene's government took steps to improve ethnic relations. Jayewardene, for example, organized a conference to try to discuss solutions and sought to form alliances with Tamil leaders. TULF responded

## LTTE TERRORISM

The government of Sri Lanka and many Sinhalese Sri Lankans regard the LTTE as terrorists rather than fighters for a Tamil homeland. The LTTE, in fact, has attacked both civilian and government targets. It also uses terrorist tactics, such as suicide bombers known as Karum Puligal, or Black Tigers. The LTTE carried out its first suicide operation on July 5, 1987, by smashing a truck filled with explosives into an army camp in Jaffna, killing forty government soldiers. Countless other suicide attacks have followed. One of the highest-profile attacks occurred in May 1993, for example, when a suicide bomber assassinated Sri Lankan president Ranasinghe Premadasa. Even President Chandrika Kumaratunga was a victim of the LTTE in December 1999. She survived, but she lost sight in one eye from the blast. One of the most daring recent LTTE operations was a mortar and suicide bomb attack on the Katunayake International Airport on July 24, 2001, that killed twenty-one people, many of them civilians. In addition, the airport was crippled when six passenger planes—half the Sri Lankan Airways fleet—and eight military planes were set on fire.

*Rows of armed soldiers in the Liberation Tigers of Tamil Eelam march during a 2002 parade. This group of radicals has been fighting for Tamil independence since the 1970s.*

by pledging to work with the government and a leader of one Tamil group, the Ceylon Workers' Congress, and even accepted a cabinet post in the UNP government. The government also made political concessions to the Tamils. Although Sinhalese remained the official language, Tamil was given a new "national language" status that expanded its legal uses. In addition, the UNP government eliminated the discriminatory university admissions policy created by the United Front government and offered many high-level government positions to Tamil civil servants.

These efforts, however, proved to be too little, too late. A number of more radical, mostly younger, and hostile Tamil separatist groups known collectively as the Liberation Tigers of Tamil Eelam (LTTE) attracted broad Tamil support and advocated armed struggle to achieve Tamil independence. Each time TULF began to cooperate with the government, LTTE would stage violent terrorist attacks against the government and its Tamil supporters. As scholar K.N.O. Dharmadasa explains, "The LTTE indulged in planned acts of violence such as robbing banks, damaging state property, and assassinating members of the police and the army as well as others, ranging from Tamil politicians who supported the two main national political parties, the UNP and the SLFP, to persons considered to be police informers."[15] These attacks inevitably provoked Sinhalese retaliation, and in this way generally destroyed any successful government peace strategy.

The government's response to the new terrorism was to pass into law the 1979 Prevention of Terrorism Act. The act authorized a state of emergency in which the Sri Lankan army, made up of mostly Sinhalese soldiers, was sent to occupy most of the northern part of the island. The legislation, however, seemed to backfire because it caused only greater resentment among Tamils as their villages were occupied and controlled by the Sinhalese.

Thereafter, ethnic violence escalated as Tamils both increased the number of terrorist attacks and began to hit more well-known targets. In one of the worst incidents, for example, Tamil terrorists ambushed and killed an army patrol of thirteen soldiers in July 1983. This attack sparked massive ethnic rioting that went on for two days. Using voter lists, Sinhalese mobs systematically located and killed Tamils and burned their houses. The mob violence started in

Colombo but quickly spread throughout the entire island. Several thousand Tamils were killed, tens of thousands were left homeless, and more than one hundred thousand fled to southern India. As Bullion explains, "It took the government nearly a week to quell the violence, which demonstrated to many observers a deliberate slowness to intervene in stopping Sinhalese violence against Tamils."[16]

Following the riots, Jayewardene's government once again turned to legislation in an attempt to gain control over the violence. In August 1983, the government adopted the sixth amendment to the constitution to ban political parties that advocated the establishment of a separate state in Sri Lanka. Like the earlier antiterrorism law, however, the amendment only worsened ethnic relations in Sri Lanka because it outlawed even the peaceful advocacy of Tamil separatism. Its effect, therefore, was to remove TULF members from the National State Assembly, the nation's legislature, because they would not take an oath promising not to promote an independent Tamil state. This closed off the peaceful legislative route for resolving the Tamil problems and led to even more intensified violent strategies. Ironically, despite Jayewardene's initial promises to remedy the ethnic problems in Sri Lanka, his government succeeded only in seriously exacerbating the country's ethnic conflict.

## THE FAILURE OF THE 1987 PEACE ACCORD

By the late 1980s, the country was in chaos and government attempts to subdue the Tamils by force or negotiate a solution to its ethnic problem were failing. Massacres were common. One massacre in May 1985 claimed the lives of 150 people (mostly Sinhalese), all of whom were gunned down by Tamil terrorists. In addition, the violence had a significant, negative effect on Sri Lanka's economy, since the terrorism destroyed businesses, caused tourism to slump badly, and forced the government to spend large sums on the military. Allegations of human rights abuse by the Sri Lankan army in its crackdown on Tamils also raised the specter of withdrawals of foreign aid.

The deteriorating situation in Sri Lanka and the migration of so many Tamils to neighboring India eventually prompted India to become involved in an effort to stabilize the region. After a series of diplomatic contacts and attempts to negotiate a solution to the conflict in Sri Lanka, Indian mediators made some headway. In July 1987, the Sri Lankan government agreed to a peace accord with India that made certain concessions to the Tamils. Basically the accord promised to provide more local autonomy for the Tamils in northern Sri Lanka through several measures: a transfer of power to the provinces; merger of the northern and eastern provinces; and the grant of official status for the Tamil language. In addition, the accord provided certain benefits to India, including military access to the port at Trincomalee. Also, as part of the peace agreement, an Indian Peace-Keeping Force (IPKF) moved into northern Sri Lanka to try to establish order and disarm the Tamils.

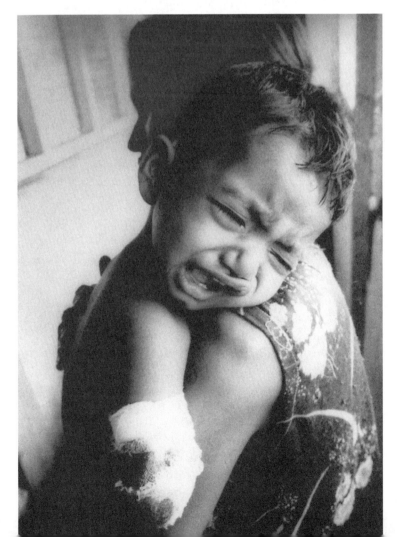

*A Tamil mother in the town of Jaffna comforts her son, whose arm was amputated after he was injured during a Sinhalese attack.*

# THE 1987 PEACE ACCORD

In 1987 India mediated negotiations that led to the Indo–Sri Lanka peace accord, an agreement designed to "devolve" (transfer) power to the Tamils in northeastern Sri Lanka in exchange for their disarmament. However, as explained by Tamil writer Nadesan Satyendra in a January 1988 article archived on the Tamil Nation Web site, the Tamils were disappointed because the agreement:

- [was signed by India and Sri Lanka to secure] the geopolitical interests of India in the Asian region. . . .

- required the Tamil militant movement to disarm even before the conclusion of negotiations. . . .

- refuse[d] to recognize the existence of a homeland for the Tamil people. . . .

- refuse[d] to structure a federal constitution where power may be shared between the Tamil nation and the Sinhala nation. . . .

- [sought] to . . . enable a Sinhala dominated Central government to control and regulate the exercise of . . . ["devolved" Tamil] power. . . .

- is content to let the provincial councils be dependent on the largesse [generosity] of a Sinhala dominated Central Government.

Although the peace accord was signed only by the Indian and Sri Lankan governments, the Tamil militant groups at first appeared ready to abide by its provisions. As time went by, however, the LTTE became increasingly resistant to disarmament and began to engage in skirmishes with IPKF forces in the north. At the same time, Sri Lankan security forces faced a violent insurgency in the south led by the People's Liberation Front (Janatha Vimukthi Peramuna, or JVP), an anti-Tamil Sinhalese extremist group that opposed the peace agreement as a betrayal of the Sinhalese. The JVP even began a campaign to kill family members of security forces if they did not lay down their arms—a strategy that backfired and eventually led to an army suppression of the JVP uprising.

By 1989 the entire country was again living in terror and the economy was on the verge of collapse, with terrorist attacks causing disruptions of transportation, strikes, and rising food prices. In the face of this escalating chaos and at the request of the Sri Lankan government, India withdrew its IPKF forces in 1990. With India's withdrawal, the Tamil problem was once again left to the Sri Lankan government, which was now headed by the UNP's Ranasinghe Premadasa, Jayewardene's successor.

## THE 2001 CEASE-FIRE AND PEACE NEGOTIATIONS

Three years of brutal civil war followed the withdrawal of Indian peacekeepers from Sri Lanka. With foreign troops gone and the JVP crushed, the Sri Lankan army could concentrate all their energies on the LTTE. As journalist William Mc-Gowen reports, "Renewed hostilities produced what Asia Watch [a human rights group] has called 'human suffering on an almost incalculable scale.' Strafing helicopters rarely distinguished between civilians and guerrillas, shelling was indiscriminate, and newly acquired heavy aircraft dropped 300 kilogram bombs that left craters twenty feet wide and ten feet deep."[17] The hostilities culminated in the assassination of President Premadasa in 1993 by a Tamil suicide bomber.

*Sri Lankan president Chandrika Kumaratunga is working to maintain the tenuous peace between the Tamil and Sinhalese.*

# OPERATION SUNSHINE

In 1995 Sri Lankan president Kumaratunga directed a military attack, called "Operation Sunshine," to retake Jaffna from the Tamils. During the assault, hundreds of innocent civilians were killed or wounded and more than five hundred thousand civilians were displaced. Political science professor A. Jeyaratnam Wilson, who witnessed the attack, describes what he saw in his 2000 book, *Sri Lankan Tamil Nationalism: Its Origins and Development in the Nineteenth and Twentieth Centuries*:

The city of Jaffna found the war on their door-step. In panic and fear the residents of the city and the outskirts—nearly half a million people—began to march out of the city on a journey without a destination, deserting their ancestral homes and lands—their world. . . . I saw parents leaving the bodies of their dead children and running to save their lives and helpless mothers letting their infants die of starvation. Not only the dead but even the sick and elderly were abandoned. . . . People wanted to cry but had no more tears left. On that day an entire community felt that even its basic human dignity was now denied them by a state that claimed to be their liberators.

*Tamils flee the city of Jaffna as the Sri Lankan army approaches during "Operation Sunshine" in 1995.*

In the following year, the Sri Lankan government seemed to abandon the notion that the Tamils could be defeated militarily, and appeared to embrace more peaceful solutions. Chandrika Kumaratunga, daughter of former prime minister Bandaranaike, was elected president. She ran as the leader of the People's Alliance (PA), a coalition that included the SLFP and some other small parties, and won the election largely by promising to negotiate with the LTTE to end the country's civil war.

Initial peace talks began in October 1994 and were greeted by mass euphoria among war-weary Sri Lankans. The peace process, however, came to a sudden end after just a couple of weeks when a suspected LTTE bomb assassinated UNP leader Gamini Dissanayake and killed fifty-six other people. Talks resumed in 1995, but once again fell apart that same year when the government, faced with continuing LTTE terrorism, sent a massive military force into the northern city of Jaffna to root out an LTTE stronghold there. The brutal offensive, called "Operation Sunshine," lasted fifty days. During the fighting, government troops killed as many as two thousand Tamils and displaced more than five hundred thousand civilians, who fled to other parts of Sri Lanka controlled by the Tamils.

The government hailed this military effort as a way to bring peace to the north, but it only further alienated the Tamils, who claimed that the government had committed atrocities against Tamil civilians. The LTTE later regrouped and again began launching damaging terrorist attacks. In December 1999, President Kumaratunga herself was caught in the blast of a suicide bomber, causing her to lose sight in one eye.

Despite the injury, Kumaratunga won the next election in 2001 and continued as Sri Lanka's president. With the help of a Norwegian mediator, Erik Solheim, the Sri Lankan government and the LTTE negotiated a cease-fire that began in February 2002. Peace talks between LTTE and the UNP government, brokered by the Norwegian delegation, were also initiated, but they broke down in 2003 when the LTTE withdrew from the talks. Today the cease-fire remains largely intact, with occasional violations limited mainly to the northern part of Sri Lanka.

Sri Lanka's government, therefore, is still struggling to end the country's prolonged civil war, as well as the side effects of that struggle—a displaced and hostile Tamil population, unemployment, high inflation, poor infrastructure, and other problems. The 2004 tsunami added to the country's woes and caused extensive damage in Sri Lanka. Yet Sri Lanka's democracy has somehow remained relatively stable, and a shaky peace still prevails, at least preserving hope for the future.

# 4

# THE PEOPLE
# OF SRI LANKA

Sri Lanka's ethnic violence stems directly from the great diversity among its people, who come from several different cultures, languages, and religions. These different cultures, instead of melding together and enriching each other over the years, have retained their distinct characteristics and separateness. Today, these differences have become almost unbridgeable, with hostile competition between the country's two main ethnic groups for political and economic power.

### THE MAJORITY SINHALESE

Sri Lanka's population of almost 20 million is made up of a number of very different ethnic groups. The most well-known ethnicities are the Sinhalese and the Tamils, participants in the country's much-publicized civil war. The Sinhalese have always formed the majority and today make up about 74 percent of the population. They claim to be direct descendants of Prince Vijaya from northern India, but they have intermarried with a variety of indigenous and immigrant peoples for centuries.

The Sinhalese are united by a shared language (Sinhala) and religion (Buddhism), yet there are divisions even among the Sinhalese. There is a marked difference, for example, between the highland Sinhalese and the lowland Sinhalese. The Sinhalese kingdom of Kandy, located in the island's highlands, remained independent of European rule until 1818, and Kandyan or highland Sinhalese therefore proudly held on to their cultural customs, religion, and beliefs, and came to think of themselves as the true Sinhalese. Meanwhile, lowland Sinhalese merged into the British culture and government, in many cases abandoning their Sinhalese customs and becoming as English as their rulers. Many of these coastal Sinhalese, for example, converted to Christianity, received a British education, and became prosperous members of the colonial society. As social scientist James Heitz-man explains, "A wider, more cosmopolitan outlook differentiated the low-country Sinhalese from the more 'old fashioned' inhabitants of the highlands."[18]

Although the Sinhalese once ruled all of the Sri Lankan island, as early as the thirteenth century A.D. they were pushed south by the Tamils, a people who had migrated to the island's northern areas. Today the Sinhalese people remain concentrated in the densely populated southwest part of Sri Lanka. Despite this concentration in one part of the country, however, the Sinhalese largely control the Sri Lankan government and military. Their culture is also the dominant one in Sri Lankan society.

## THE TAMILS

The Tamils are Sri Lanka's second-largest ethnic group. Altogether, they account for about 18 percent of the total population of the island. They speak a completely different language (Tamil) from the Sinhalese and follow a different religion

*This girl and her family are Sinhalese, the ethnic group comprising nearly 75 percent of Sri Lanka's population.*

(Hinduism). Unlike the Sinhalese, whose ancestors traveled from northern India, Tamils hail from southern India.

There are two distinct groups of Tamils living in Sri Lanka—the Ceylon Tamils and the Indian Tamils. The Ceylon Tamils are descended from people from southern India who have lived on the island for centuries. Like the Sinhalese, they see Sri Lanka as their ancestral home. They number about 12.7 percent of the total population of the island, are full citizens of the country, and live mostly in the northern and eastern parts of the island. During British rule, many Ceylon Tamils attended British schools and either worked for the colonial government or held well-paid positions in fields such as medicine and engineering. The Indian Tamils, on the other hand, are descendants of poor people from southern India who were brought by the British to Sri Lanka in the nineteenth century to work on the country's tea and rubber plantations. Most Indian Tamils settled near Sri Lanka's tea-growing areas in the country's south-central region, where they earned very little and lived in substandard conditions. Today the Indian Tamils form about 5 percent of the Sri Lankan population, and most continue to live in the highlands area.

*These boys playing in a fountain are Indian Tamils, whose ancestors were brought to Sri Lanka by the British.*

# VELUPILLAI PRABHAKARAN, LTTE LEADER

Velupillai Prabhakaran has been the leader of the Tamil rebel group known as the Liberation Tigers of Tamil Eelam (LTTE) for more than twenty years. He operates from a secret base somewhere in the jungles of northeastern Sri Lanka and has a reputation as a fearless and ruthless guerrilla fighter. Many Tamils see him as a freedom fighter, but to the government of Sri Lanka, he is a terrorist. He rarely appears in public, but in a March 1986 interview with the *Week Magazine*, Prabhakaran explained the reasons for his fight against the Sri Lankan government:

It is the plight of the Tamil people that compelled me to take up arms. I felt outraged at the inhuman atrocities perpetrated against an innocent people. The ruthless manner in which our people were murdered, massacred, maimed and the colossal damage done to their property made me realize that we are subjected to a calculated program of genocide. I felt that armed struggle is the only way to protect and liberate our people from a totalitarian Fascist State bent on destroying an entire race of people.

*From his secret base in northeastern Sri Lanka, Velupillai Prabhakaran has led the LLTE since the 1980s.*

Many of the Ceylon Tamils have long considered themselves superior to the poorer and lower-class Indian Tamils, and social divisions still remain. Since the outbreak of armed conflict between the government and Tamil rebels in the mid-1980s, for example, the Indian Tamils have generally not participated in the fight for Tamil independence. Instead they have been represented by a separate group, the Ceylon Workers' Congress (CWC). Members of the CWC have held posts in the Sinhalese-dominated government since the 1970s. Even today, the CWC is part of the coalition government of President Kumaratunga.

Instead of fighting for independence, Indian Tamil leaders have fought for greater civil rights within Sri Lanka. For example, they have pushed for wage increases, better educational opportunities, and citizenship rights, which were denied them soon after independence in the citizenship acts of 1948 and 1949. In 1988 Sri Lanka granted citizenship to about 230,000 of these stateless Indian Tamils. Still, as many as 75,000 Indian Tamils remain in Sri Lanka as noncitizens. The government has promised not to force them to return to India, and in October of 2003, granted citizenship to several thousand more Tamils. Those who remain stateless are not allowed to vote and cannot hold jobs in the government.

The war has caused several hundred thousand Tamils to flee from Sri Lanka. At the end of 2000, approximately 65,000 Tamils were still living in 131 temporary refugee camps in southern India, and as many as 200,000 more lived elsewhere in India. Another 200,000 Tamils reportedly have sought refuge in Western countries. Many of these exiled Tamils are eager to return to Sri Lanka as soon as hostilities end and conditions are safe.

### THE MOORS AND THE MALAYS

Besides the Sinhalese and the Tamils, Sri Lanka also is home to several less-numerous ethnic groups. The largest of these are two Muslim groups, the Moors and Malays, which together constitute about 7 percent of the country's total population. The Moors can be further divided into Sri Lankan Moors and Indian Moors. The Sri Lankan Moors trace their ancestry to Arab traders who moved to southern India and Sri Lanka between the eighth and fifteenth centuries. This group, which makes up most of the Muslim community, lives in the central highlands according to Islamic law and speaks a type of Arabic-Tamil that contains a large number of Arabic words. The Indian Moors, on the other hand, are Muslims who came to Sri Lanka to obtain work during the colonial period. They came from places such as Sind (today part of Pakistan) and northwestern India, and continued to speak their native languages. Today they number only several thousand people.

The Malays are Muslims from Southeast Asia whose ancestors came to Sri Lanka during the Dutch colonial period. Most were brought to the island to work as soldiers for the colonial government, but some were convicts or nobles who were exiled from Indonesia. They speak the Malay language with the addition of both Tamil and Sinhalese words. The

Malay population is quite small, composing only about 5 percent of the Muslim population in Sri Lanka.

## THE BURGHERS AND THE VEDDAS

Yet another tiny ethnic group, making up only about 0.3 percent of the total population, is the Burghers, descendants of European colonists from Portugal, the Netherlands, and Britain who intermarried with indigenous people but historically clung to their European ancestry. During colonial times, they lived near Colombo and dominated the top government positions. Following independence, Burgher families began to lose their status and influence in Sri Lanka and many have since migrated to places such as nearby Australia.

*An indigenous Vedda or Wanniyalaeto man sits on a street in Colombo with betel nuts in his lap.*

Finally Sri Lanka is still home to about twenty thousand people known as Veddas (Sinhalese for "hunters") or Wanniyalaeto (forest dwellers). These are the descendants of the ancient inhabitants of Sri Lanka, who have lived on the island since 16,000 B.C., long before the arrival of the Sinhalese. Although this community has experienced successive waves of immigration and colonization, they have survived and maintained their ancient culture by retreating farther and farther into Sri Lanka's interior forest region. Veddas have a strong attachment to the forest; as one Vedda leader explains, "I was born in the forest. My ancestors come from here. We are the forest beings, and I want to live and die here. And even if I were reborn only as a fly or an ant, I would still be happy so long as I knew I would come back to live here in the forest."[19]

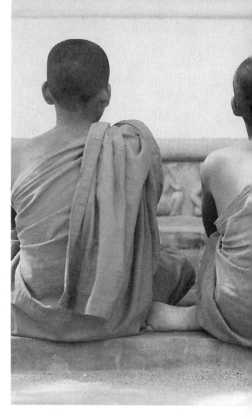

Today, however, deforestation threatens Vedda lands and many Vedda have been absorbed into Sinhalese or Tamil society. Only a few Vedda remain who continue to live the traditional forest-dwelling lifestyle. The Vedda community, however, is working with the Sri Lankan government to place the Maduru Oya National Park under Vedda control and management, in order to help preserve this indigenous culture. As a Vedda Web site explains, "Unless measures are taken soon, . . . the indigenous human culture that successfully managed the forest environment for millennia face[s] almost certain extinction."[20]

## BUDDHISM IN SRI LANKA

Sri Lanka's ethnic groups embrace very different religions. Most Sinhalese are Buddhist, for example, and today Buddhists are estimated to account for about 70 percent of the modern Sri Lankan population. Buddhism teaches the ways of the Buddha, a man called Siddhārtha Gautama, who lived twenty-five hundred years ago in northern India. At the age of thirty-five, he is said to have gained enlightenment (called nirvana), the highest spiritual state human beings can reach in the Buddhist religion. The Buddha's main teachings are that suffering is caused by attachments to the world, and that enlightenment is achieved by releasing these attachments. Daily meditation is the key Buddhist spiritual practice. A large number of Buddhist shrines exist to promote meditation, reverence for the Buddha, and prayers to a number of gods for help with daily life. Buddhist disciples, called monks, preserve Buddha's teachings and practices.

In Sri Lanka, Buddhism has been intricately involved with the country's politics. Since independence, the Sinhalese majority has united around the religion and promoted it as a central part of true Sri Lankan identity. Even Buddhist monks have attended rallies, fasted in protest, and otherwise become involved in worldly politics. As Heitzman notes, "[The monks'] high status in the eyes of the Sinhalese population, gave the Buddhist orders influence as molders of public opinion."[21] Indeed, the country's constitution, while ensuring freedom of religion, contains special protections for Buddhism that fall just short of declaring it an official state religion.

In recent years, a growing number of Buddhist extremists have begun pushing to make Sri Lanka officially a Buddhist state in which the principles of Buddhism would be applied to all citizens. These extremists have also historically opposed efforts to settle differences with the Tamils and have on occasion harassed Christians, even burning some Christian churches. In 2003, for example, the U.S. State Department reported that there were over one hundred serious attacks against Christian churches, pastors, or congregations. A surge of anti-Christian attacks by Sinhalese mobs was also reported in late 2004.

*With their heads shaved and wearing orange robes, these young Sinhalese boys live in a Buddhist monastery where they will one day become monks.*

## HINDUISM, CHRISTIANITY, AND ISLAM

Most Tamils are followers of Hinduism. Unlike Buddhists, Hindus do not follow one specific religious figure, and there is no organized Hindu religious order. Many Hindus do, however, accept the Buddha as an important spiritual teacher, but not the only one. One of Hinduism's deepest beliefs is the concept of nonviolence. The cow, for example, symbolizes life and motherhood to Hindus and is considered a sacred animal that should not be killed. Hindus also believe in reincarnation, the idea that a person comes back to live a new life after death in a new body unconscious of his or her previous lives. Like Buddhists, Hindus visit temples, where they pray and make offerings to a number of different gods. Some of the most important Hindu gods are Vishnu, who manifests both as the heroic Rama and the warrior god Krishna; Vishnu's wife Lakshmi, who governs wealth and good fortune; and Shiva, a powerful god with divine and earthly qualities. Shiva is often called "the Destroyer" and is highly popular among Tamils.

In addition to the two main religions, Hinduism and Buddhism, Sri Lanka is also home to Christians and Muslims. Sri Lanka's Christians constitute only about 8 percent of the population of the country. They include both Sinhalese and Tamils, as well as Burghers. Most Christians follow the Roman Catholic branch of Christianity, brought to the island centuries ago by the Portuguese. Many Christians in the past were associated with the colonial government, and today Christians still live primarily in the southwestern lowlands. Most of Sri Lanka's Muslims, the Moors and the Malays, follow a branch of Islam known as Sunni Islam. Muslims believe in one God (called Allah) and follow the teachings of the Koran, Islam's holy book.

## LANGUAGES

The country's two main ethnic groups also each have their own unique language. Sinhala, a language spoken by the Sinhalese, is an Indo-European language that has its roots in northern India. Today Sri Lanka is the only place where Sinhala is spoken. The Veddas, who no longer speak a language of their own, also speak Sinhala. Tamils and most Muslims, on the other hand, speak Tamil, part of the South Indian Dravidian linguistic group. This language existed in southern India before the Indo-European speakers arrived in northern India, and although it has adopted many Indo-European words over the years, it has retained much of its original Dravidian essence. It is still spoken not only in Sri Lanka but also by more than 40 million people in southern India.

Like religion, language has played a pivotal role in Sri Lankan politics. During British rule, for example, English was designated the official language and became the language used in government, business, and schools. After independence, however, English was considered by Sri Lankans to be a symbol of colonialism, leading the government to replace it with Sinhala as the country's official language. This decision

## WOMEN OF SRI LANKA

In many ways, the status of women in Sri Lanka has greatly improved since colonial times. Today women have much greater access to education, and many have entered politics or other government employment. Recent economic reforms, such as free-trade zones and other free-market policies, have contributed to an increase in jobs. As a result, Sri Lankan women today are employed in a variety of jobs, from positions as factory workers to managers. Indeed, garment manufacturing and foreign employment are the two biggest earners for the country, and women produce most of this income. Sri Lanka also has a female president and many female cabinet ministers.

However, household chores and child care are still considered primarily women's responsibility, and violence against women is on the rise. Many of the women employed

in low-level positions, such as garment workers or maids in Middle Eastern homes, work long hours and are sexually exploited by their employers. They also often must leave their children without proper care, a situation that is contributing to a high level of incest and social upheaval in Sri Lanka.

*Sri Lankan female workers in Colombo make lace by hand for clothing and furnishings.*

to create only one official language helped to precipitate the ethnic conflict between the Sinhalese and the Tamils, who thought that the Tamil language should be given equal weight. Today both Sinhalese and Tamil are the official languages for their respective ethnic groups.

The government lately has been trying to reintroduce and encourage the use of English, both because it is important in the global economy and because its use could help reduce frictions between the two main ethnic groups. Today, however, English is spoken only by about 10 percent of the population—mainly by middle and upper-middle classes, especially people who live and work in Colombo, the nation's capital.

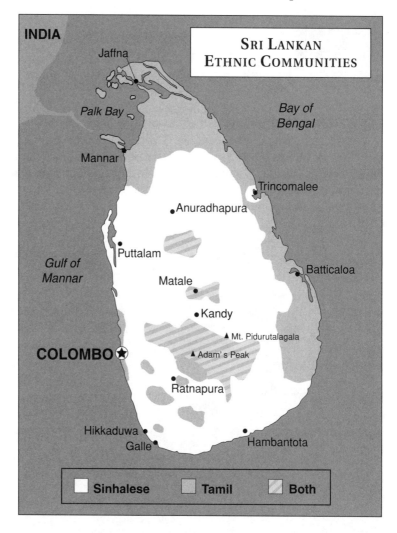

## ETHNIC SEGREGATION IN SRI LANKA

One of the most noticeable features of Sri Lankan society is the physical and cultural segregation of its different ethnic groups. These groups live in certain, specific areas of the island depending largely on where their ancestors settled. The Sinhalese, for example, are concentrated in the central, southern, and western regions, while the Ceylon Tamils occupy most of the north and east, especially the area around the Jaffna Peninsula. The Indian Tamils live primarily in the highlands, near the tea and agricultural areas. The Muslims, meanwhile, can be found in large concentrations on the northwest coast and in certain east coast districts. The only place where members of all of these ethnic groups live together is in Colombo, the country's capital city and main urban area. Here a Sinhalese majority live and work with sizable groups of Tamils and Muslims as well as with Burghers and Malays.

Even in Colombo, though, the various ethnic communities live in different neighborhoods and associate largely with people from their own ethnic group. Children are separated from each other starting in primary school, where they are taught in either Sinhala or Tamil. Businesses, too, tend to serve their particular ethnic group by advertising in one language or the other. Other aspects of society are likewise segregated by custom and language. Sports teams, for example, are usually made up of only one ethnic group.

The ethnic divisions are fed by people's fears that other ethnic groups may try to dominate and repress their culture, religion, and language. As Heitzman explains, "The Sinhalese are the overwhelming majority of residents within Sri Lanka, but they feel intimidated by the large Tamil population in nearby India. . . . The Sinhalese feel quite isolated as the only group in the world speaking their language and professing their variant of . . . Buddhism."[22] Most Sinhalese also believe the Tamils enjoyed an overly privileged position under British rule, and that despite their small numbers, today unfairly control almost one-third of the land in Sri Lanka. The Tamils, however, as a minority in Sri Lanka, fear that the Sinhalese, with their current hold on the nation's government and power, want to eliminate or absorb the Tamil culture and restrict Tamils' educational and work opportunities. Other even smaller minorities, such as the Muslims, seek to hold their own in the middle of this Sinhalese and Tamil competition.

### CULTURAL SIMILARITIES IN SRI LANKAN SOCIETY

Despite their many differences, however, most Sri Lankans share certain cultural characteristics, perhaps because so many of their ancestors came from various parts of India. One similarity among all Sri Lankans is their love of family and children. In all ethnic groups, marriage and the nuclear family are highly valued and divorce is rare. Children are doted upon, and close contacts are kept with extended family members. Most Sri Lankans also share many similar social values such as hospitality, politeness, and cleanliness.

Another important similarity between the Sinhalese and the Tamils is the caste system, a custom associated with India and Hinduism. In this system, each person is born into a particular group, or caste, that defines one's fixed position in society and often determines one's occupation. Among the Sinhalese, the main caste is the Goyigama, traditionally an elite group that held royal positions and owned land. Members of this caste today still dominate the political scene and

## EDUCATION IN SRI LANKA

Following Sri Lanka's declaration of independence in 1948, the government gave a high priority to improving the national education system. These efforts largely succeeded, producing a literacy rate of 93 percent. Today school is compulsory for children from five to thirteen years old and provided free by the government. The government also pays for higher levels of education, even at the university level. Students choose to be instructed either in the Sinhala or the Tamil language, and English is taught as a second language. Sri Lanka has thirteen universities, all of them public. The largest universities are also the oldest and include the University of Colombo (founded in 1921); the University of Peradeniya (founded in 1942 in Peradeniya, a suburb of

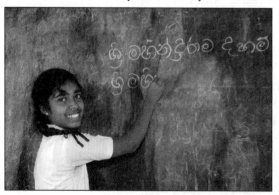

Kandy); and the University of Sri Jayawardenepura (founded in 1958 in Sri Jayaardenepura, just outside Colombo). In addition, Sri Lanka has medical schools, engineering schools, schools of law, and technical and vocational training schools.

*The Sri Lankan government places a premium on education, and the country enjoys an extraordinarily high literacy rate.*

tend to be among the wealthiest people in Sri Lankan society. Various other castes lie below the Goyigama. In fact, some castes are so low that higher caste groups consider them "untouchable" and unfit to participate in religious and social functions. Traditionally, this designation of the untouchables has forced some people to live as virtual outcasts within the society.

The Tamil caste system is similar to that of the Sinhalese. The dominant Tamil caste, for example, is the Vellala. Many Ceylon Tamils belong to this Vellala caste, and the Vellala have historically dominated Tamil commercial and educational elites, particularly in the Jaffna region. The Indian Tamils, on the other hand, are mostly members of very low castes from southern India; this accounts for their isolation, both in the society at large and within the Tamil community.

The caste systems of both groups, however, have undergone changes in recent years, and people today generally go about their business without regard to caste inequalities. This is particularly true in urban areas. As the travel Web site Sri Lanka Tour explains, "Members from different castes have to cluster on buses together with few worries about the 'polluting' of their purity; they eat or talk together freely in restaurants or in companies they work together. Employment, health, and educational opportunities are officially open to all without the prejudice based on caste system."[23] Yet caste considerations are sometimes still important in Sri Lankan society. Particularly in rural areas, villages are still divided into separate neighborhoods by caste, and many families disapprove of their children marrying someone in another caste.

Just as caste divisions are becoming less significant to many Sri Lankans, more and more of the nation's citizens are hoping that other traditional divisions will fade. Those who are tired of civil war and ethnic strife look forward to a time when the country's sparring ethnic groups will be able to focus more on their commonalities than on their differences. Only then, many believe, will the state and its people become truly united.

# 5

# Sri Lankan
# Arts and Culture

Although Sri Lanka's mix of different ethnic groups has clearly produced great discord and violence for the country, it also has created a rich, diverse, and very interesting culture. Indeed, Sri Lanka is known for its ancient cultures and exquisite arts, many of which express religious themes or ideas. Indian Buddhism, in particular, has played a significant role in the country's culture. Today, however, these ancient influences exist side by side with newly emerging modern ideas and art forms.

### The Importance of Dance

One of the most important ancient Sri Lankan arts is dance. The Sinhalese have three main classical dance forms, all of which are based on folk religions that existed on the island even before the Sinhalese adopted the Buddhist religion. In fact, Sri Lankan dance began as part of ancient religious rituals and ceremonies that were held to influence the gods to prevent natural disasters, provide good harvests, and cure illnesses. As Sri Lankan Internet writer Hemasiri Premawardene explains, "[This] pre-Buddhistic folk religion consisted of the belief in a variety of deities and demons who were supposed to be capable of awarding benefits and blessings but also causing afflictions and diseases. Accordingly, they had to be either propitiated [appeased] or exorcised with offerings and the performance of rituals and ceremonies."[24] The old rituals and ceremonies are rarely conducted today, but the classical dances associated with them are still performed, mostly for entertainment purposes. These dance performances are very elaborate; the dancers display great agility, athleticism, and acrobatics, and use heavy symbolism and ornate costuming.

Perhaps the most well-known Sri Lankan classical dance style is high country, or Kandyan, dance. It developed in the ancient Kandy kingdom and is still practiced among the highlands near the city of Kandy. Kandyan dance is the national dance of Sri Lanka and has become famous as a tourist attraction. Kandyan dancers wear elaborately decorated costumes and perform to the beat of drums called *gata beraya*. Although there are five different types of Kandyan dance, the *ves* dance is the most popular. The *ves* dancers wear very elaborate and highly decorated costumes, including headgear. The *ves* dance originated in an ancient purification ritual called *kohomba kankariya*. It is considered highly sacred and can only be performed by males. Once, this dance was only permitted to be performed within temples, but today it has become known as the epitome of classical Kandyan dance.

Another classical dance form, the low country or Ruhunu dance, is a ritual dance in which dancers wear masks to depict various characters such as birds, demons, or reptiles. It is performed to appease the folk god Devol Maduwa and exorcise demons that cause a variety of incurable illnesses. For

*A traditional dancer in elaborate costume leads a procession in Colombo. Sri Lankan dance has its roots in ancient religious ceremonies.*

# SRI LANKAN SPORTS

For leisure, Sri Lankans often play traditional games or sports. Games of skill and mock combat, field games, and water sports have all been played since ancient times on the island. One of the most popular organized sports in Sri Lanka today, however, is cricket, a legacy of British colonial rule. Cricket is played throughout Sri

Lanka by all ethnic groups, and the Sri Lankan cricket team is highly ranked internationally. In 1996 Sri Lanka defeated Australia in the final of the Wills World Cup, a major cricket championship. Another British sport is golf, a sport played by wealthy English planters and governors during colonial days as part of an effort to re-create the English lifestyle in Sri Lanka. Other Sri Lankan sports include rugby, cycling, tennis, and motor events. Running has also become a favorite sport. In the 2000 Sydney Olympics, Susanthika Jayasinghe, who has been described as Sri Lanka's wonder girl, made history by becoming the first Sri Lankan woman to win an Olympic medal. She won the bronze medal in the women's two-hundred-meter finals, missing the silver by only 0.01 seconds.

*Runner Susanthika Jayasinghe celebrates after winning a bronze medal at the 2000 Olympics in Australia.*

this reason, Ruhunu dancers are sometimes called "devil-mask dancers." A third dance type, the Sabaragamuwa dance, is also a religious dance. It is performed with drums, to honor the folk god Gam Maduwa in order to ensure a good harvest, ward off evil, or eliminate infectious disease. This dance comes from the province of Sabaragamuwa, located near Colombo.

The Tamils also have their own classical dances. These dance styles originated as part of sacred Hindu ceremonies in southern India and represent the elements of air, water, and fire. The classical Tamil fire dance *bharata-natyam*, for example, is a highly stylized dance performed by one female dancer whose movements are supposed to resemble those of a dancing flame. The Tamil classical dances, like the Sinhalese classical dances, are today performed not only in temples but also at festivals and other venues, primarily for entertainment.

In addition to classical dance forms, Sri Lankans also enjoy folk dances. One of the Sinhalese folk dances, for example, is the *leekeil*, a dance in which each dancer knocks two sticks together to create rhythm. There is also a low country Sinhalese tradition of folk dance-theater, which includes the *kolam*, a masked drama performed to amuse and provide social satire, and the *sokari* and *nadagam*, stylized dramas accompanied by singing. A popular Tamil folk dance is the *karakattam*, a religious dance performed in front of the goddess Mariamma. The dancer holds a brass pot filled with uncooked rice on his or her head, and dances to a folk song without spilling any of the rice. Folk dances are typically performed at the country's many festivals and similar community activities.

## DRUMS AND MUSIC

Like its dances, much of Sri Lanka's music is rooted in tradition and religion. Indigenous music usually features drums and percussion as the leading instruments. In fact, the drum is Sri Lanka's national instrument and is used in many different events, including not only dances but also dramas, religious celebrations, weddings, funerals, and other rites of passage. Certain families in Sri Lanka have become known for providing generations of this music. As music educator Robert G. Smith explains, "The family of low country musician Herbert Dayasheela claims over twenty generations of famous Sri Lankan musicians. The family even owns copyright of a number of ancient pieces of music and dances which they still perform."[25] Much of this percussive music is very complex and challenging to perform. One of the best places to hear the music is the annual Buddhist Perahera festival in the city of Kandy.

Folk songs are also quite popular in Sri Lanka. The range and variety of these folk musical styles is great, and there are folk songs about almost every type of rural activity. For example, there are Sinhalese harvest songs (*kamath gee*), rice planting songs for women (*netelim gee*), lullabies (*daru nelavili*), game and dance songs (*keli gee*), and many others. One very popular folk song—"Maloo, Maloo, Maloo"—has simple lyrics about fish brought fresh from the sea. However, it is often sung at social gatherings with lyrics spontaneously created to poke fun at friends or satirize politicians. The Tamils also have their versions of folk tunes.

Despite the continued popularity of traditional and folk music, however, Sri Lankans are also increasingly influenced by more contemporary styles. Much of the country's native pop music is rooted in *baila*, a type of music that originated with African slaves brought to the island by the Portuguese in the fifteenth century. *Baila* began as vocals accompanied by guitar or hand clapping. Modern Sri Lanka pop music, however, employs electric guitars, synthesizers, and other instruments. Another popular type of music is Indian *filmi*, which is known for its poetic lyrics. Many young Sri Lankans, too, are embracing Western pop music, and the variety of influences is creating a unique and vibrant musical scene in the nation.

## RELIGIOUS, COLONIAL, AND MODERN ARCHITECTURE

The island's architecture is also heavily influenced by religion and history but has felt the impact of modern styles. Probably the most dominant architectural element seen throughout Sri Lanka is the Buddhist dagoba or stupa—a dome-shaped plaster building, often painted white, that was primarily used to enshrine the Buddha's relics such as hair, bones, and teeth. Today the stupa is still used everywhere in the country to create places of devotion and contemplation. Statues of the Buddha are often found in these structures, as well as fresco paintings depicting beautiful women, deities, or temple dancers. Ancient examples of this Buddhist structure can be found at the Anuradhapura and Polonnaruwa ruins. The Ruwanweliseya, or the "Great Stupa," at Anuradhapura, for example, stands 300 feet (91.4m) high and is considered one of the country's most important religious structures.

Hindu temples, called *kovils*, are also part of Sri Lanka's religion-based architecture. The temples typically have a dome or pyramid shape and are elaborately decorated both inside and outside with bright colors and low-relief sculptures. The temples also usually have two rooms, a prayer hall and a

*Hindu temples like the Nallur Kandaswamy Temple in Jaffna are intricately decorated.*

shrine room, both dedicated to the Hindu god Shiva. One of the most impressive and popular Hindu temples in Sri Lanka, the Nallur Kandaswamy Temple, is located in Jaffna. Built in A.D. 948, it is considered an excellent example of Dravidian art.

Sri Lanka's architecture was also affected by the region's long colonial legacy. Portuguese influences, for example, can still be seen in Portuguese tile roofs and long verandas (or porches), as well as in the structure of many Catholic churches. Dutch flavor is most evident in the country's old Dutch forts and canals. The British style is most easily seen in British residences, clubs, and courthouses. Galle, located in southern Sri Lanka, is known as the finest colonial city on the island. Its main attraction is a 90-acre (36.4ha) Dutch fort—a walled city built in the seventeenth century that contains many grand old Dutch residential houses and churches. One of the best-preserved Dutch structures in Galle is the Great Church, built in 1752 and featuring beautiful gables and stained-glass windows.

## TEMPLE OF THE TOOTH

The Temple of the Tooth, called Dalada Maligawa, is undoubtedly the most revered Buddhist shrine in all of Sri Lanka. The temple was originally built around A.D. 1600 by Kandyan king Vimaladharmasuriya but has since been modified and rebuilt. Today it is an intricately designed and decorated structure made of white plaster, with courtyards, an octagonal tower, numerous murals and sculptures, and even a moat. Ac-

cording to legend, this temple houses one of the Buddha's teeth, said to have been smuggled to Sri Lanka after the Buddha was cremated in India. The tooth was first housed at Anuradhapura but was brought to the Kandyan kingdom in 1592.

*Buddhists believe that the ornate Dalada Maligawa temple in Kandy is home to the Buddha's tooth.*

Although Sri Lanka is steeped in these ancient influences, modern architects are also building fine structures in Sri Lanka. One of the most influential, prolific, and award-winning of Sri Lanka's modern architects, for example, is Geoffrey Bawa. Bawa has combined Western architectural styles with Sri Lankan needs, creating a bridge from Sri Lanka's past to the present. Bawa's design of the Sri Lankan Parliament building in Colombo, for example, features a contemporary style that interprets ancient architectural forms in a modern way.

## PAINTINGS AND SCULPTURE

The importance of keeping tradition alive in Sri Lanka is also evident in sculpture and painting. For example, dotted throughout Sri Lanka are statues and sculptures of the Buddha. In ancient times, these statues were often carved directly into limestone cliffs found throughout the islands. During more recent times, they have been sculpted from a variety of valuable materials including jade, crystal, marble, emerald, ivory, coral, wood, and metal. The Buddha is typically shown in one of three poses: standing, meditating, or reclining. One of the best places to see truly exquisite Buddha sculptures is in the country's numerous Buddhist shrines. Some the Buddha sculptures are colossal. For example, a free-standing sculpture in Aukana, near Anuradhapura, towers 42 feet (12.8m) high. In another series of sculptures carved from a granite ridge in Polonnaruwa, a standing Buddha is 23 feet (7m) tall, and a reclining Buddha there is 46 feet (14m) long.

Traditional Sri Lankan paintings also often relate to the Buddha, either depicting his life or his prior lives. Excellent paintings can be seen on the walls of Buddhist monasteries and shrines. These are usually in one of two distinct styles—either classical or Kandyan. The classical period, which lasted from about the fifth century to the thirteenth century, produced paintings that were more ornate and expressive than later artwork. The earliest and most impressive classical paintings, called frescoes, were painted on plaster walls and depicted beautiful and voluptuous women, as well as the Buddha. During the Kandyan period, which began in the eighteenth century, paintings became more simplified and were produced mainly to provide ornamentation for Buddhist temples during a time of Buddhist religious revival.

*This fifth-century fresco at Sigiriya depicts a woman carrying flowers on a tray.*

Colors are limited to red, yellow, white, black, blue, and green, and compositions are simple.

However, Sri Lanka is also home to more contemporary, nonreligious art. This modern art was at first influenced by European art traditions that were introduced by the British in the latter part of the nineteenth century. This changed, however, in mid-century, when artists became more independent in their style. As Sri Lankan artist Anoli Perera explains, "The 1940s and 1950s marked the most significant period in the history of painting and sculpture in 20th century Sri Lanka."[26] The changes began in 1943, when a group of artists known as the 43 Group began to challenge the restrictions of imitating Victorian art. These artists fused bright, indigenous color schemes and drawings with Western and Indian art traditions to create a brand new form of secular and wholly Sri Lankan painting. Some of the 43 Group painters who became well-known during this time included George Keyt, Justin Daraniyagala, Richard Gabriel, and Ivan Peries. The modernist styles created by the 43 Group continue to have significant influence on Sri Lankan art. The National Art Gallery in Colombo is the country's main art museum. It showcases a permanent art collection and holds exhibitions of various modern Sri Lankan artists.

## LITERATURE

Like other arts, writing began in Sri Lanka as a religious activity but has evolved into more modern forms. The country's literary tradition dates back over two thousand years, beginning with the *Mahavamsa*, the great chronicle of early Sinhala kingdoms written by Buddhist monks around 500 B.C. This record was written in Pali, a Buddhist language. Later, however, Sinhala developed as a literary language, as shown by Sinhala prose and poetry etchings found on the walls of Sigiriya, a rock fortress dating back as early as the seventh century A.D. Beginning in about 1200, poems about the lives of the Buddha were composed in the Sinhala language.

The Tamils also have a long literary tradition with an emphasis on poetry. The earliest known Sri Lankan Tamil poet was Eelattu Poothanthevanar, who wrote in southern India before A.D. 250. In the 1940s, the works of Tamil renaissance poets Mahakavi, Kandasamy, and Varadar established a distinctly Sri Lankan Tamil literary tradition that separated Sri Lankan poetry from that produced by Tamils in southern India.

Fiction has been a part of Sri Lanka's literature since the early 1900s. Martin Wickramasinghe was one of the country's first modern Sinhalese novelists. He wrote about social changes that occurred toward the end of colonialism in Sri Lanka. Today both Sinhala and Tamil writers produce

## SRI LANKAN TV, RADIO, AND INTERNET

Sri Lanka's media, like its society, is divided along ethnic lines. The government owns many of the main media outlets, including two major TV stations, radio networks operated by the Sri Lanka Broadcasting Corporation (SLBC), and various newspapers. These state-owned companies broadcast and publish in three languages—Sinhala, Tamil, and English. Sri Lanka also is home to privately owned media companies, including over a dozen radio stations and eight TV stations. These companies have the freedom, under Sri Lanka's laws, to criticize government policies. In 2002 the government even permitted Tamil rebels to legally broadcast radio programs from their Voice of Tigers radio station in northern Sri Lanka. The Internet is also a growing source of news and current events in Sri Lanka. Press freedoms, however, have been threatened by the ongoing conflict; deaths threats and murders of journalists have been common.

a variety of poetry and fiction. Some of these include Jean Arasanayagam, Ann Ranasinghe, and Romesh Gunesekera, whose works focus on the effects of ethnic strife and war in Sri Lanka. Other award-winning Sri Lankan writers are Michael Ondaatje and Shyam Selvadurai, both of whom now live in Canada but write about their experiences in Sri Lanka.

## HANDICRAFTS

Handicrafts are another highly developed ancient art form in Sri Lanka that has found a contemporary niche. Today many different types of crafts are produced, including various wood carvings, weavings, pottery, lace, canework, and metalwork. The island, however, is especially known for its masks, batik fabrics, and jewelry. Sri Lanka's masks, for example, were traditionally used in rituals and dances, but today they are a recognized art form. They are made from a lightweight wood called *kaduru* and carved into various characters. The three main categories of masks are *sanni, kolam*, and *raksha*. *Sanni* means "sickness," so these masks were originally made to drive away disease. *Kolam* masks are used mostly in dramas in southern Sri Lanka, and *raksha* masks typically are carved in the shapes of cobras, peacocks, and mythical birds.

Batik, colorful fabric made by using wax to create elaborate dye patterns, is actually an Indonesian art, but has been developed by Sri Lankans into an original style. The patterned fabric is made by a tedious process that begins with a line drawing on white cloth or silk. Melted wax is then carefully dripped onto parts of the cloth that are not to receive dye color. The fabric is dyed, and then the process is sometimes repeated several times with various colors to produce highly intricate designs. These fabrics are highly popular with tourists.

Sri Lanka also produces excellent quality costume jewelry in one of two styles—the Galle tradition and the Kandyan tradition. The Galle, or low country, tradition is characterized by an emphasis on the use of precious stones, with very little metal showing. This jewelry is similar to Western types of jewelry. The more traditional Kandyan jewelry, in contrast, features intricate metalwork as the main decoration. One Kandyan technique, for example, uses filigree—the welding of delicate silver wire the thickness of human hair onto a silver surface.

### SRI LANKAN CUISINE

The cuisine of Sri Lanka is as refined as some of Sri Lanka's other arts and crafts, but influenced largely by Indian tastes. As in India, Sri Lankan food is characterized by fiery hot dishes that are tempered by rice and terrific teas. Rice and curry dishes with vegetables, meat, or fish are the most typical food. The basic Sri Lankan curry is made with coconut milk, sliced onion, green chili, and spices such as cloves, nutmeg, and cinnamon.

Meals are often accompanied by items such as *parripu* (a red lentil dish), *mullung* (stir-fried green leaves with spices), and *sambol* (a mixture of grated coconut, chilis, and spices). Another unique Sri Lankan specialty is *hoppers*, a type of flat pancake made from rice flour that is eaten for breakfast or a snack. It is often served with fried eggs, yogurt, or sweetened coconut. Coastal towns are also known for their delicious, fresh fish, especially tuna.

A boy stands next to a string puppet in Ambalangoda, an area known for its elaborate puppets and masks.

Typical desserts include *kiribath*, a rice dish cooked in coconut milk; *kevum*, a spice cake; and *kiri peni*, made from yogurt curd and honey. Tea, grown in Sri Lanka, is the most popular beverage, and fruit is usually served at the end of the meal. Local tropical fruits include mangoes, papayas, passion fruit, and bananas, to name just a few.

*An elephant, richly decorated for the religious festival of Perahera, carries a ceremonial chair through the streets of Kandy.*

## FESTIVALS

For leisure, Sri Lankans often attend the country's many bright and colorful festivals. Most festivals are related to religion, but there are also secular holiday traditions. Not surprisingly, there are numerous Buddhist festivals. The Duruthu festival in January, for example, marks the first visit of the Buddha to Sri Lanka. Another festival called Vesak, held in May, marks the birth, enlightenment, and death of the Buddha. Other Buddhist festivals commemorate the day Buddhism was introduced into Sri Lanka (Poson) and the day a sapling from the sacred bo tree in India was brought to Sri Lanka (Unduvap).

Although Buddhist festivals dominate the calendar, other religions also have their celebrations. The main Hindu festivals are Vel, a celebration held in July and August to honor the war god Skhanda, and Deepavali, a festival of lights held in October and November to celebrate a Hindu legend about the victory of good over evil. Muslims also have their festivals, but these are less public. The major Muslim events are the Milad-un-Nabi (held in December), marking the birth of the Prophet, and Id-ul-Fitr (held in October), marking the end of the holy fasting during the month of Ramadan.

Probably the most colorful and exciting nonreligious festival, however, is the traditional New Year festival, a national holiday celebrated by both the Sinhalese and the Tamils, but in very different ways. For the Sinhalese, this holiday occurs in April each year and features an elaborate weeklong festival period. As the travel Web site Sri Lanka Tour describes it, "The festival . . . coincides with the end of the harvest season and the beginning of the new season. People enjoy the brand new day of the New Year by cleaning their house, buying their new clothes, and eating special meal[s] in a union of family members."[27] The Tamils, however, celebrate the New Year on the first day of the year, and only for a few hours.

Sri Lanka is a country steeped in religious arts and traditions. Yet these ancient traditions have begun to mix freely with contemporary influences, creating an even more fascinating Sri Lankan culture.

# 6

# SRI LANKA AT
# A CROSSROADS

Sri Lanka is blessed with great beauty, abundant natural resources, and a refined culture. It has managed to triumph
over colonial rulers and establish an independent nation and
government. Yet the small island is still the site of a simmer-
ing civil war and a struggling economy, and many of its people are in great need due both to the fighting and the recent
tsunami trauma. The country is thus at a crossroads; its future is uncertain, and its people face both tremendous challenges as well as opportunities.

## TSUNAMI RECOVERY
Tsunami recovery, observers say, must be Sri Lanka's most
immediate goal. The tsunami was the worst natural disaster
in recent human history. Although it took more than two
hours from the time of the earthquake for the waves to hit Sri
Lanka, residents still received no warnings. When the
tsunami finally arrived, it struck with great ferocity. Wit-
nesses in Trincomalee reported seeing waves as high as 40
feet (12.2m) washing half a mile (0.8km) inland. The giant
waves hit almost all of Sri Lanka's coastlines, destroying
whole communities and wiping out roads, bridges, houses,
schools, hospitals, and clinics. In the end, the tsunami killed
more than forty thousand Sri Lankans and left more than a
million homeless. The northeastern Tamil areas, already ravaged by the country's civil war, were especially hard hit.
Thousands of people there had already been displaced by
the country's ethnic fighting and were living in temporary
camps, only to face nature's fury when the tsunami struck.

The tsunami also caused significant economic damage. It
wiped out two-thirds of Sri Lanka's fishing fleet and shattered
the country's tourist industry. Before the disaster, the tourist
industry had just begun to benefit from the cease-fire between Tamil rebels and the government. Following the 2002

cease-fire, for example, the number of tourists had increased in 2003 to a record five hundred thousand, with an even higher number in 2004. Now some observers say it may take a decade for the tourist industry to regain its previous heights. Overall, experts predict that economic growth will likely slow significantly in 2005 as a result of the tsunami damage. Fortunately, however, the tsunami did not affect the country's economic mainstays, plantation crops and garment manufacturing.

After the tragedy the government, relief agencies, and the people of Sri Lanka immediately focused on providing relief to the injured and the homeless. The government quickly announced a tsunami recovery plan focusing on humanitarian assistance and rebuilding. President Kumaratunga also asked the churches for help in caring for the large number of newly orphaned children. Because of the many years of civil war, the churches have had plenty of practice taking care of victims, and they know how to work with both sides of the armed conflict. In Tamil areas, the LTTE also used its tough military discipline to quickly mobilize teams of workers to search for survivors and provide basic shelter, first aid, and counseling.

*In the city of Galle, a small damaged statue of Buddha sits amid a pile of rubble in the aftermath of the December 2004 tsunami.*

Soon, humanitarian aid began to filter in from international relief organizations.

Sri Lanka, however, cannot afford to pay the huge costs of these recovery efforts and much of the money will have to come from international loans and grants. The Sri Lankan government estimates that the total cost of recovery will come to $3.5 billion. Analysts suggest that at least $200–300 million will be necessary for the humanitarian assistance alone, and repairing the infrastructure will likely cost an additional $1.6 billion, with further rebuilding costs still to be calculated. Fortunately, the International Monetary Fund (IMF), an international economic aid group, quickly agreed to an emergency loan of $157.5 million to Sri Lanka. Millions more in loans and grants have been pledged by other coun-

## PRESIDENT KUMARATUNGA'S PLEA

On February 4, 2005, Sri Lanka's first Independence holiday following the 2004 tsunami, President Chandrika Kumaratunga addressed the nation:

The occurrence of the morning of [December 26, 2004] . . . is the most terrible . . . experience that Sri Lankans have [ever experienced]. In one hour the fury of nature destroyed hundreds of thousand of lives. . . . Not only were many centuries of our sweat and effort ravaged but also a significant portion of our history. . . . The mighty forces of nature have taught us a lesson. . . . The ocean . . . made no difference between Sinhala or Muslim or Tamil. . . . In one indiscriminate sweep the mighty forces of nature taught us that man is equal everywhere and that we have to stand together if we are

to successfully meet the challenges posed by mother nature herself, leave alone disasters that we have generated for ourselves such as conflicts and wars. I appeal to all Sri Lankans . . . to massively change our thinking and our attitudes . . . in order that we rebuild our Nation into a modern progressive and truly Sri Lankan State.

*President Chandrika Kumaratunga calls on the people of Sri Lanka to band together and help rebuild the country after the tsunami.*

tries, organizations, and individuals eager to help with the longer term tsunami recovery.

## ENVIRONMENTAL DAMAGE

In addition to creating a human and economic tragedy, the deadly tsunami also knocked down trees, damaged beaches, and left Sri Lanka's marine areas clogged with debris that could cause serious damage to the island's coral reef systems. Furthermore, the saltwater waves scattered wildlife and contaminated freshwater ponds, wells, and other water supplies. After the tsunami, the island's heavily populated coastlines looked completely obliterated, with virtually nothing left standing. Human debris such as bits of clothing, pieces of cars and boats, and chunks of concrete and wood were strewn everywhere.

However, the extent of the environmental damage from the tsunami was actually much less than many experts expected, especially in undeveloped areas where the energy of the waves was diluted by sand dunes, healthy coral reefs, and mangrove trees. As M.A. Sanjayan, the lead scientist of the Nature Conservancy, reported after surveying the environmental damage, "The good news is that the physical impact of the tsunami was limited and the coral is relatively intact. . . . The bad news is that post-tsunami impacts, such as debris washed into the ocean, are high and unless we clean it up immediately, damage will continue to accrue."[28] Sanjayan's recommendations to the government of Sri Lanka therefore emphasized the immediate removal of debris from the ocean and preventing people from using the ocean as a dump for other debris items as recovery efforts begin.

Moreover, Sanjayan urged that all reconstruction efforts be required to protect the environment. Specifically, Sanjayan recommended sustainable redevelopment, by which developers leave natural barriers such as sand dunes, mangroves, and reefs alone when building near the coasts. In addition, Sanajayan suggested that tourism and fishing along Sri Lanka's coast should be regulated to prohibit overfishing, boats dropping anchors on coral reefs, coral mining, and other damaging activities. As Sanjayan explained,

In many ways, the tsunami gave us a chance to realize the damage that is taking place and to change bad

behavior. . . . Many of the resources we assessed would
have been destroyed in a few decades even if the
tsunami hadn't hit. Hopefully aid money will not only
be spent to reconstruct people's lives, but also to ensure
the sustainability of their livelihoods by protecting the
natural resources people depend upon.[29]

## ECONOMIC CHALLENGES

The tsunami may also create unexpected opportunities for
Sri Lanka's struggling economy. For years, the government
had been deregulating, privatizing, and opening the economy to international competition in an effort to attract in-
vestors and improve the country's economic performance.
As a 2005 U.S. State Department paper explains, "In recent
years, the [Sri Lankan] government has eliminated many
price controls and quotas, reduced tariff levels, eliminated
most foreign exchange controls, and sold more than 55 state-
owned companies and 20 estate-holding companies."[30]

These efforts to improve the economy, however, were often disrupted by ethnic violence. Although the cease-fire
with the Tamils had helped to bring some measure of stability to the country over the last couple of years, Sri Lanka's
economy before the tsunami hit was still on the verge of cat-
astrophe. Economic troubles included a record trade deficit
caused by rising oil prices in 2004, inflation as high as 15 percent, drops in the value of Sri Lanka's currency, and an aging
infrastructure that was crippling economic growth. On top of
these problems, billions of dollars in promised foreign assistance had failed to materialize because there was no movement toward peace.

Perhaps surprisingly, experts say that the tsunami will ultimately kick-start the economy by pumping millions of
dollars into reconstruction efforts. As reporter Nick Carraway asserts, "The Indian Ocean tsunamis . . . caused un-
precedented damage, but were also a blessing to [Sri
Lanka's] economy."[31] Analysts predict that, after an initial
dip in gross domestic product in 2005, the massive assistance from across the globe will be a mighty engine that will
create economic growth of more than 5 percent starting as
early as 2006. The disaster will also allow Sri Lanka to re-
structure its debt payments, freeing up more funds for de-

velopment and easing the debt burden on the country's annual budget. Alastair Corera, vice president of a global economic rating agency, explains, "This is the opportunity for growth for Sri Lanka. . . . The much-needed long term economic pick-up can start happening if the government adopts the right approach."[32]

Economists see long-term infrastructure projects, in particular, as important for stabilizing Sri Lanka's economy, and these projects will later produce even greater economic benefits by moving the country's goods more efficiently. Experts caution, however, that fiscal restraint and reforms, such as improving tax collections and imposing higher interest rates, must be continued despite the ravages of the disaster in order to increase revenues and stem inflation. Experts say other economic reforms are equally important. For example, Sri Lanka must still work to reduce the country's budget deficit, pay down its loans, and diversify the economy beyond its two main exports, tea and textiles. So far the biggest growth has been in the service industries, such as tourism,

*Displaced Sri Lankans repair their tsunami-damaged homes in Hikkaduwa, south of Colombo.*

financial services, and telecommunications, and there also is a small information technology sector. In addition, economists urge the government to improve education and jobs. The country's unemployment rate has declined in recent years, but it still hovers near 9–10 percent. The government also has implemented educational reforms to try to better prepare students for available jobs.

The future of Sri Lanka's economy, experts say, depends on this tsunami relief and these continued economic reforms. However, maintaining the peace process and increasing political stability, economists admit, are also key to this economic recovery process.

### THE STRUGGLE FOR PEACE

With the economy seemingly poised for a comeback, perhaps the biggest worry for Sri Lanka continues to be whether the two decades of civil war can be ended in a manner that keeps the country united, stabilizes the economy, and begins to heal the deep wounds created in Sri Lanka's society. So far, as many as sixty-four thousand people have died in the twenty-year conflict, and over forty thousand have been displaced from their homes and farms. Peace talks have been suspended since 2003, when LTTE withdrew from negotiations. Since then a cease-fire has held, although there have been sporadic violations by both sides.

Most of the post-cease-fire violence, however, has actually been caused by power struggles within the LTTE. In March 2004, a Tamil commander in the east, Colonel Karuna, rebelled against the leadership of Velupillai Prabhakaran, the head of the LTTE; thereafter, over 150 of Karuna's supporters have been killed, presumably by mainstream LTTE fighters loyal to Prabhakaran. In turn several senior LTTE leaders have also been assassinated, probably by Karuna's followers. Notably the LTTE accuses the government of providing military aid and intelligence to the Karuna group.

Shortly after the tsunami, there was hope that the disaster might bring the warring sides in Sri Lanka together. The sheer breadth and scope of the damage caused by the disaster made fighting virtually impossible, bringing complete peace to the area for the first time in decades. Both President Chandrika Kumaratunga and the leader of LTTE's political wing, Suppah Paramu Thamilchelvam, called for national unity in public statements, and the two sides began to coordinate their disaster efforts. A glimmer of hope was created for the first time in years. As Thamilchelvam explained to reporters in early January 2005, "National emergencies sometimes create statesmen."[33]

As relief efforts began, however, it became clear that the disaster would only exacerbate tensions between the government and the Tamils. Squabbles began almost immediately over the distribution and allocation of aid as Tamil leaders accused the government of holding up aid to the northern areas. Many of the problems were caused because foreign aid could not be distributed directly to the LTTE, which the United States and other countries view as a terrorist organization, and therefore had to be channeled through the Sri Lankan government.

The Sri Lankan government and the Tamils discussed setting up a joint relief mechanism to distribute the aid, but government officials split on the issue, making aid distribution

## LTTE's Interim Peace Proposal

Since 2003 the LTTE has been insisting that government peace negotiators consider their proposal for an interim Tamil authority to govern the northeast until a permanent peace agreement is reached. The interim proposal provides, in part, for an Interim Self-Governing Authority (ISGA) to be established in the Tamil area of northeast Sri Lanka. The majority of members of the ISGA would be appointed by the LTTE, but members would also be appointed by the government of Sri Lanka and the Muslim community. If a permanent agreement resolves the current ethnic conflict within five years, it would then take the place of the interim plan. If no final settlement is reached within seven years, however, the interim proposal provides that elections would be held to elect members to the ISGA, and the ISGA would continue governing the northeast region. Other parts of the interim proposal provide ground rules for the ISGA government. These include, for example, human rights and antidiscrimination protections (prohibiting discrimination on the basis of religion, race, caste, national or regional origin, age, and gender) for the people of the region, as well as provisions to prevent government corruption.

yet another point of contention between the two sides. Some observers accused the Tamils of deliberately overstating the aid problems. The Tamils, these observers claim, were using the disaster merely as an opportunity to make contacts within the international community and draw the world's attention to their ambitions for independence. As reporter Bay Fang concluded, "On the island nation of Sri Lanka in the Indian Ocean, the December 26 tsunami may have swept away families and homes, but the hostilities and distrust brought on by 20 years of civil war remain."[34]

Still, neither side appears ready to restart the civil war. At the same time, there is no movement toward negotiation. The standstill surrounds the issue of the scope of the talks, with the LTTE insisting that discussions center on their proposal for an Interim Self-Governing Authority (ISGA), which would give the Tamils full authority to govern the northeastern part of Sri Lanka and provide them with a portion of the national budget. The government, on the other hand, is interested in broadening the talks to discuss an ultimate resolution that will keep the country united. As the British magazine the *Economist* explains, "The government fears the interim authority will pre-empt the final outcome, and turn into a new platform for a Tiger [LTTE] bid for full statehood."[35]

The renewed tensions following the tsunami have caused many observers to fear that without a strong government push for negotiations, the island could slide back into war. Such a result would be catastrophic, not only for Sri Lankan people who have already suffered greatly from the violence, but also for the country's economy and overall prosperity, which would be damaged by instability. Indeed, even a continued stalemate could dampen the country's tsunami rebuilding efforts and continue to affect the willingness of other countries to invest in Sri Lanka.

## POLITICAL UNCERTAINTY

Experts say the biggest obstacle to peace may be divisions within Sri Lanka's government concerning how to deal with the Tamil insurgency. After Sri Lankan president Ranasinghe Premadasa was assassinated by a Tamil rebel in 1993, the next president, Chandrika Kumaratunga, vowed to restore peace to the country. Despite these promises, however, con-

*In 2003 Prime Minister Ranil Wickremesinghe prepares to release a white dove to mark the first anniversary of the cease-fire agreement between the government and Tamil rebels.*

flict continued, and in December 1999 she herself was wounded in a Tamil terrorist attack. Kumaratunga was re-elected for a second term as president in 2001 but suffered a political setback when the UNP won big in parliamentary elections and her political opponent, UNP leader Ranil Wick-remesinghe, took office as the country's prime minister. Prime Minister Wickremesinghe made efforts to restart ne-gotiations and favored giving concessions, if necessary, to the Tamils to end the conflict, but the president has blocked

# EFFECTS OF THE CEASE-FIRE

Most Sri Lankans are exhausted from the country's civil war and are disappointed that the government has failed to take advantage of the 2002 cease-fire to negotiate a lasting peace for Sri Lanka. Jayadeva Uyangoda, a political science professor at the University of Colombo, in an article published March 16, 2005, in the *Sri Lanka Daily Mirror*, explained his view:

> What has then the three years of cease-fire added to the progress of Sri Lanka's politics? It has made returning to war quite difficult for both the state and the LTTE, although there may be a lot of temptation in both camps to unilaterally break the cease-fire agreement. It has also demonstrated that the Sri Lankan ethnic conflict has reached a qualitatively new phase in which violence and war [are] no longer necessary to mediate the relations between the state and the Tamil community. . . . The challenge ahead for Sri Lanka is to contain the spreading violence and prevent it undermining the CFA [Cease-fire Agreement]. There are signs that in all sides the commitment to protect the CFA has been weakening. The CFA gave the Sinhalese political class the necessary breathing space to resolve the conflict in partnership with the LTTE, but they seemed to have squandered the opportunity. Not even the unprecedented natural disaster of the December tsunami has moved them in a constructive direction.

*In 2005 a woman in Colombo walks by a banner urging the people of Sri Lanka to continue supporting the cease-fire.*

his peace efforts. The two politicians could not seem to find a way to work together on the country's problems.

In February 2004, seeking to erode the power of the prime minister, President Kumaratunga dissolved parliament and called for elections. In the elections, Kumaratunga's party won enough seats in parliament to allow her to bring in a new prime minister from her own party, Mahinda Rajapakse. These results eased the political power struggle and allowed

President Kumaratunga to assemble a ruling coalition. However, bickering within Kumaratunga's new coalition government has continued to prevent a unified strategy for peace.

Specifically, Kumaratunga and her United People's Freedom Alliance (UPFA) coalition party are under great pressure from one member of their coalition, Janatha Vimukthi Peramuna (JVP), Sri Lanka's main extremist Sinhalese group, to oppose any type of government concession to the LTTE Tigers. According to observers, Kumaratunga and the UPFA as of 2005 appear willing to discuss the Tamils' ISGA proposal, which seems to be the key to moving forward with negotiations. The JVP, however, holds enough seats in parliament (thirty-nine) to prevent such an effort. The disagreements have created a political deadlock in Sri Lanka.

Because President Kumaratunga is so constrained by the fervently anti-Tamil JVP, some observers fear that the fragile peace process will only continue to disintegrate. In February 2005, Kumaratunga warned JVP that it should leave her government if it continued to obstruct her efforts. If JVP does leave the governing coalition party, however, the president's power would be significantly reduced because she would only have the support of a minority of the legislature. In any event, President Kumaratunga's term expires in December 2005, and under Sri Lanka's current constitution she cannot run again. Some observers speculate that Kumaratunga may try to amend the constitution to gain the right to run for another term, but another likely scenario is that Sri Lanka will hold elections for a new president in the near future. The fragile peace process may have to wait until then for its rejuvenation.

Sri Lanka is therefore at a critical stage in its history, in which decisions made now could affect whether the country's future will be peace or war, prosperity or poverty, stability or divisiveness. Sri Lankans and their friends around the world hope for leaders who will make wise choices.

# FACTS ABOUT
# SRI LANKA

## GEOGRAPHY

Location: Southern Asia, island in the Indian Ocean, south of India

Total area: 25,332 square miles (65,610 sq.km); land: 24,996 square miles (64,739sq.km); water: 336 square miles (870sq.km)

Comparative area: Slightly larger than West Virginia

Coastline: 831 miles (1,337km)

Climate: Tropical monsoon: northeast monsoon (December to March); southwest monsoon (June to October)

Terrain: Mostly low, flat to rolling plain; mountains in south-central interior

Natural resources: Limestone, graphite, mineral sands, gems, phosphates, clay, hydropower

Land use: Arable land, 13.86%; permanent crops, 15.7%; other, 70.44% (2001 estimate)

Natural hazards: Occasional tsunamis, cyclones, and tornadoes

## PEOPLE

Population: 19,905,165 (July 2004 estimate)

Age structure: 0–14 years: 24.8% (male 2,526,143; female 2,414,876); 15–64 years: 68.2% (male 6,589,438; female 6,976,487); 65 years and over: 7% (male 655,636; female 742,585) (2004 estimate)

Birth rate: 15.88 births/1,000 population (2004 estimate)

Death rate: 6.47 deaths/1,000 population (2004 estimate)

Infant mortality rate: 14.78 deaths/1,000 live births (2004 estimate)

Life expectancy: Total population: 72.89 years; male: 70.34 years; female: 75.57 years (2004 estimate)

Fertility rate: 1.88 children born/woman (2004 estimate)

Ethnic groups: Sinhalese 74%; Tamil 18%; Moor 7%; Burgher, Malay, and Vedda 1%

Religions: Buddhist 70%, Hindu 15%, Christian 8%, Muslim 7% (1999 estimate)

Languages: Sinhala (official and national language) 74%, Tamil (national language) 18%, other 8%; [Note: English is commonly used in government and is spoken competently by about 10% of the population]

Literacy rate for those age 15 and over: total population, 92.3%; male, 94.8%; female, 90% (2003 estimate)

## GOVERNMENT

Country name: Democratic Socialist Republic of Sri Lanka (short form: Sri Lanka)

Form of government: Republic

Capital: Colombo [Note: Sri Jayawardenepura (Kotte), a suburb of Colombo, is the legislative capital]

Administrative divisions: 8 provinces: Central, North Central, North Eastern, North Western, Sabaragamuwa, Southern, Uva, Western [Note: North Eastern province may have been divided in two—Northern and Eastern]

National holiday: Independence Day, February 4

Date of independence: February 4, 1948 (from Britain)

Constitution: Adopted August 16, 1978

Legal system: A highly complex mixture of English common law, Roman-Dutch, Muslim, Sinhalese, and customary law

Suffrage: 18 years of age, universal

Executive branch: Chief of state—President Chandrika Bandaranaike Kumaratunga (since November 12, 1994) [Note: Mahinda Rajapakse (since April 6, 2004) is the prime minister; the president is considered both the chief of state and head of government]; Cabinet—appointed by the president in consultation with the prime minister; Elections—president elected by popular vote for a six-year term; election last held December 21, 1999 (next election to be held December 2005)

Legislative branch: Unicameral Parliament—225 seats; members elected by popular vote on the basis of a modified proportional-representation system by district to serve six-year terms; elections last held April 2, 2004 (next elections to be held by 2010)

Judicial branch: Supreme Court; Court of Appeals—judges for both courts are appointed by the president

## ECONOMY

Gross Domestic Product (GDP): $73.7 billion (2003 estimate); real growth, 5.5% (2003 estimate); GDP per capita, $3,700 (2003 estimate); GDP composition: agriculture 19.9%, industry 26.3%, services 53.8% (2003 estimate)

Labor force: 7.17 million (2003 estimate)

Population below poverty line: 22% (1997 estimate)

Unemployment rate: 8.4% (2003 estimate)

Industries: Rubber processing, tea, coconuts, and other agricultural commodities; clothing, cement, petroleum refining, textiles, tobacco

Agricultural products: Rice, sugarcane, grains, pulses, oilseed, spices, tea, rubber, coconuts; milk, eggs, hides, beef

Exports: $5.269 billion (2003 estimate)

Imports: $6.626 billion (2003 estimate)

Debt: $10.52 billion (2003 estimate)

Economic aid recipient: $557 million (1998 estimate)

Currency: Sri Lankan rupee (LKR)

# NOTES

## INTRODUCTION: FALL FROM PARADISE

1. Charles Jeffries, *Ceylon: The Path to Independence.* New York: Praeger, 1963, p. 3.

## CHAPTER 1: AN ISLAND JEWEL

2. Lonely Planet, "Destination Sri Lanka," 2004. www.lonely planet.com/destinations/indian_subcontinent/sri_lanka.

3. Living Heritage Trust of Sri Lanka, "Sri Pada: Myth, Legend, and Geography." http://sripada.org/index.htm.

4. Sri Lanka Tour, "Beaches," 2003. www.sri-lanka-tour. com/attraction/index.html.

5. Charlie Furniss, "Devoted to Conservation: Scientists in Sri Lanka Have Drawn Inspiration from History and Teamed Up with Buddhist Monks in an Attempt to Spread Environmental Awareness and to Put into Practice a Progressive Form of Forest Management," *Geographical*, February 2004, p. 22.

6. Travellers Worldwide, "About Colombo," November 5, 2004. www.travellersworldwide.com/09-srilanka/09-srilanka-about.htm.

## CHAPTER 2: SRI LANKA'S COLONIAL PAST

7. Peter R. Blood, "Historical Setting," *Sri Lanka: A Country Study*, ed. Russell R. Ross and Andrea Matles Savada. Washington, DC: Federal Research Division, Library of Congress, 1992, p. 15.

8. Jeffries, *Ceylon: The Path to Independence*, p. 5.

9. Blood, "Historical Setting," p. 31.

10. Jeffries, *Ceylon: The Path to Independence*, p. 34.

11. Sri Lanka Tour, "Sri Lanka History," 2003. www.sri-lanka-tour.com/history/independence.htm.

## Chapter 3: Independence and Civil War

12. Blood, "Historical Setting," p. 43.

13. Alan J. Bullion, *India, Sri Lanka and the Tamil Crisis 1976–1994: An International Perspective*. New York: Pinter, 1995, p. 23.

14. Quoted in Bullion, *India, Sri Lanka and the Tamil Crisis 1976–1994*, p. 13.

15. K.N.O. Dharmadasa, *Language, Religion, and Ethnic Assertiveness: The Growth of Sinhalese Nationalism in Sri Lanka*. Ann Arbor: University of Michigan Press, 1992, p. 316.

16. Bullion, *India, Sri Lanka and the Tamil Crisis 1976–1994*, p. 32.

17. William McGowen, *Only Man is Vile: The Tragedy of Sri Lanka*. New York: Farrar, Straus and Giroux, 1992, p. 377.

## Chapter 4: The People of Sri Lanka

18. James Heitzman, "The Society and Its Environment," *Sri Lanka: A Country Study*, ed. Russell R. Ross and Andrea Matles Savada. Washington, DC: Federal Research Division, Library of Congress, 1992, p. 73.

19. Quoted in South Asian Media Net, "People of Sri Lanka." www.southasianmedia.net/profile/srilanka/srilanka_people.cfm.

20. Vedda.org, "Sri Lanka's Vedda or Wanniyaleato." http://vedda.org.

21. Heitzman, "The Society and Its Environment," p. 95.

22. Heitzman, "The Society and Its Environment," p. 80.

23. Sri Lanka Tour, "Society of Sri Lanka." www.sri-lanka-tour.com/travel-guide/society.htm.

## CHAPTER 5: SRI LANKAN ARTS AND CULTURE

24. Hemasiri Premawardene, "Dances of Sri Lanka," Lanka Library. www.lankalibrary.com/rit/dance2.htm.

25. Robert G. Smith, "Sri Lankan Music," Dr. Bob Smith Music Educator, February 18, 2005. http://members.iinet.net.au/~bobsmith/sri.htm.

26. Anoli Perera, "State of Sri Lankan Art," *Frontline*, February 13–26, 1999. www.flonnet.com/fl1604/16040660.htm.

27. Sri Lanka Tour, "Festivals in Sri Lanka," 2003. www.sri-lanka-tour.com/travel-guide/festivals.htm.

## CHAPTER 6: SRI LANKA AT A CROSSROADS

28. Quoted in the Nature Conservancy, "First Environmental Survey of Tsunami Damage Shows Sri Lankan Coasts and Forests Hurt but Rebounding," February 24, 2005. http://nature.org/pressroom/press/press1797.html.

29. Quoted in The Nature Conservancy, "First Environmental Survey of Tsunami Damage Shows Sri Lankan Coasts and Forests Hurt but Rebounding."

30. Bureau of South Asian Affairs, U.S. Department of State, "Background Note: Sri Lanka," February 2005. www.state.gov/r/pa/ei/bgn/5249.htm.

31. Nick Caraway, "Tsunami a Blessing in Disguise for Sri Lanka's Economy," Free Republic, February 8, 2005. www.freerepublic.com/focus/f-news/1338722/posts.

32. Quoted in Caraway, "Tsunami a Blessing in Disguise for Sri Lanka's Economy."

33. Quoted in Melinda Li, "Sri Lanka: Getting Relief to Tiger Territory," *Newsweek*, January 17, 2005, p. 32.

34. Bay Fang, "Keeping a War on Hold?" *U.S. News & World Report*, January 24, 2005, p. 24.

35. *Economist* (US), "As Good as It Gets? Sri Lanka's Peace Process," October 16, 2004, p. 40.

# CHRONOLOGY

**5th century** B.C.
Prince Vijaya arrived on the island of Sri Lanka with a group of settlers from northern India.

**437** B.C.
Pandukabhaya, a Sinhalese King, founds Anuradhapura, a powerful city-state on Sri Lanka.

**3rd century** B.C.
Buddhism is introduced and spreads throughout the island.

**200–100** B.C.
The Tamils, a people from southern India, invade the Sinhalese kingdoms.

**A.D. 10th century**
The Cōla empire from southern India invades Sri Lanka, destroys Anuradhapura, and moves the island's capital to Polonnaruwa.

**1153–1186**
The Sinhalese regain control of Polonnaruwa under King Parakramabahu.

**13th century**
The Tamil Hindus control the northern part of the island, forcing the Sinhalese into the southern and central regions.

**1505**
The Portuguese discover the island and, over the next century, gain control over the northern Tamil kingdom of Jaffna and the southern Sinhalese kingdom of Kotte. The kingdom of Kandy holds out against the Portuguese.

**1612**
Dutch traders agree to help the king of Kandy fight the Portuguese in exchange for a monopoly on the spice trade.

**1656**
The Portuguese surrender to the Dutch, and the Dutch jointly rule the island together with the Kandy kingdom for the next century.

**1796**
The British seize the port of Trincomalee and oust the Dutch from the entire island.

**1830s**
The British establish large agricultural plantations on the island to grow coffee; they import cheap Tamil laborers from southern India to work on the plantations.

**1833**
The Colebrook-Cameron Commission recommends reforms in the British colonial system; as a result of the commission, the British overseers place all parts of the island under one government and create educational and work opportunities for Sri Lankans.

**1870**
A disease devastates the coffee industry, and planters switch to tea and rubber crops, requiring the Indian Tamils to settle permanently on the island.

**Early 1900s**
Educated Sri Lankans begin to press for greater representation in the colonial government.

**1948**
On February 4, colonial rule ends and the island nation of Ceylon becomes an independent nation.

**1948–1949**
Citizenship legislation takes away voting rights from the Indian Tamils.

**1956**
The Sri Lankan Freedom Party (SLFP) wins elections and S.W.R.D. Bandaranaike becomes prime minister. The new government makes Sinhala the sole official language.

**1958**
A rumor that a Tamil killed a Sinhalese sparks riots that

leave hundreds of Tamils dead and more than twenty-five thousand relocated away from Sinhalese areas.

## 1960
After Bandaranaike is assassinated in September 1959 by a Buddhist extremist, his wife, Sirimavo, becomes prime minister.

## 1965–1970
The United National Party (UNP) rules and implements the Tamil Language Regulations, permitting the Tamil language to be used for certain official purposes in Tamil areas. The law causes Sinhalese protests.

## 1970–1977
Sirimavo Bandaranaike returns as prime minister.

## 1972
The government adopts a new constitution that makes Buddhism the country's primary religion, changes Ceylon's name to Sri Lanka, and declares the country to be a republic.

## 1973
The government implements a discriminatory policy that makes university admissions criteria easier for Sinhalese than for Tamils.

## 1970s
In response to Bandaranaike's anti-Tamil policies, the Tamils found the Tamil United Liberation Front (TULF), which demands an independent Tamil state of Tamil Eelam. Later in the decade, an even more radical Tamil group, the Liberation Tigers of Tamil Eelam (LTTE), is formed and advocates armed struggle to achieve Tamil independence.

## 1977
The UNP, led by Junius Richard Jayewardene, wins elections and takes steps to ease tensions between the Sinhalese and the Tamils.

## 1978
Jayewardene's government changes the constitution to replace the parliamentary-style government with a new government system that gives the president more power. Jayewardene becomes Sri Lanka's president.

**1979**
Following increasing LTTE terrorist attacks on people and property, the government enacts the Prevention of Terrorism Act, under which the Sri Lankan army is sent to occupy Tamil areas.

**1982**
Jayewardene is reelected as president.

**1983**
Tamil terrorists ambush and kill an army patrol, sparking massive ethnic rioting across the island that kills and displaces thousands of Tamils, and causes more than one hundred thousand to flee to southern India. In response, the government adopts a sixth amendment to the constitution to ban parties that advocate a separate Tamil state.

**1980s**
Tamil violence increases and the government responds with force.

**1987**
The Sri Lankan government agrees to a peace accord with India that provides the Tamils more local autonomy and grants official status for the Tamil language. An Indian Peace-Keeping Force (IPKF) arrives in northern Sri Lanka to establish order and disarm the Tamils.

**1990**
India withdraws its IPKF after rising violence from both LTTE and an extremist Sinhalese group, the People's Liberation Front (Janatha Vimukthi Peramuna, or JVP).

**1991**
The civil war escalates, leading to the assassination of President Ranasinghe Premadasa, Jayewardene's successor, by a Tamil militant.

**1994**
Chandrika Kumaratunga, daughter of former prime minister Bandaranaike, is elected president as the leader of the People's Alliance (PA); she initiates peace talks with LTTE. The talks fail after UNP leader Gamini Dissanayake is assassinated by LTTE.

**1995**

Peace talks resume but again end when the government orders Operation Sunshine, a military operation in Jaffna to root out LTTE fighters.

**1999**

President Kumaratunga is attacked by a suicide bomber. The blast blinds her in one eye but does not kill her.

**2001**

Kumaratunga wins a second term as president but the UNP wins parliamentary elections, allowing UNP leader Ranil Wickremesinghe to become prime minister.

**2002**

With the help of a Norwegian mediator, Kumaratunga negotiates a cease-fire with LTTE.

**2003**

Peace talks break down when LTTE withdraws.

**2004**

In April, President Kumaratunga dissolves parliament and Kumaratunga's party wins enough seats in parliament to allow appointment of a new prime minister, Mahinda Rajapakse.

**2004**

In December, Sri Lanka is hit by a massive tsunami that kills forty thousand Sri Lankans and leaves a million homeless.

**2005**

President Kumaratunga warns the JVP that it should leave her government if it continues to obstruct her peace efforts.

# FOR FURTHER READING

## BOOKS

Krishnan Guruswamy, *Sri Lanka*. Milwaukee, WI: Gareth Stevens, 2002. This children's book examines the history, geography, people, government, economy, art, and recreation of Sri Lanka.

Nanda Pethiyagoda Wanasundera, *Cultures of the World: Sri Lanka*. New York: Benchmark, 2002. A young-adult book that reviews Sri Lanka's geography, history, government, economy, environment, culture, and society.

Robert B. Zimmerman, *Sri Lanka*. Chicago: Children's, 1992. A juvenile selection that describes the geography, history, culture, industry, and people of Sri Lanka.

Lawrence J. Zwier, *Sri Lanka: War Torn Island*. Minneapolis, MN: Lerner, 1998. A book for children that provides an unbiased picture of the people and groups involved in Sri Lanka's civil war.

## WEB SITES

**Lonely Planet** (www.lonelyplanet.com/destinations/indian_subcontinent/sri_lanka). A travel Web site that contains useful information about various aspects of life and travel in Sri Lanka, including discussions of the country's history, culture, and environment.

**Tamil Nation** (www.tamilnation.org/conflictresolution/tamil eelam/norway/contents/14.htm). A Web site run by the Tamil rebels that provides information about the peace process and proposals from the Tamil point of view.

**U.S. Central Intelligence Agency (CIA)** (www.cia.gov/cia/ publications/factbook/geos/ce.html). This U.S. government Web site gives geographical, political, economic, and other information on Sri Lanka.

**U.S. Department of State** (www.state.gov/r/pa/ei/bgn/52 49.htm). A U.S. government Web site providing an up-to-date overview of Sri Lanka's people, history, government, economy, political conditions, and foreign relations.

# WORKS CONSULTED

## BOOKS

Alan J. Bullion, *India, Sri Lanka, and the Tamil Crisis 1976–1994: An International Perspective.* New York: Pinter, 1995. A study of the relationship between India and Sri Lanka, with an emphasis on the Indo–Sri Lankan peace accord of 1987 and events leading up to the 1994 election.

K.M. De Silva, *A History of Sri Lanka.* Berkeley: University of California Press, 1981. A scholarly history of Sri Lanka, from ancient times to the mid-1970s, written by a preeminent Sri Lankan historian.

K.N.O. Dharmadasa, *Language, Religion, and Ethnic Assertiveness: The Growth of Sinhalese Nationalism in Sri Lanka.* Ann Arbor: University of Michigan Press, 1992. An exploration of Sinhalese nationalism and the role of language and religion in Sri Lanka's ethnic relations.

Charles Jeffries, *Ceylon: The Path to Independence.* New York: Praeger, 1963. A story of Britain's connection with Ceylon and its path from a British colony to independence, written by a member of the British Colonial Office.

William McGowen, *Only Man Is Vile: The Tragedy of Sri Lanka.* New York: Farrar, Straus and Giroux, 1992. A journalist's account of the conflict between the Sinhalese and the Tamils in Sri Lanka.

Russell R. Ross and Andrea Matles Savada, eds., *Sri Lanka: A Country Study.* Washington, DC: Federal Research Division, Library of Congress, 1992. A Library of Congress study and report on Sri Lanka that provides a good overview of its history, society, economy, government, military, and foreign policy.

A. Jeyaratnam Wilson, *Sri Lankan Tamil Nationalism: Its Origins and Development in the Nineteenth and Twentieth Centuries.* Vancouver, CAN: UBC, 2000. A study of the Tamils' history and culture that traces the development of Tamil nationalism up to its present-day military stance.

## PERIODICALS

*Australasian Business Intelligence,* "Rebuilding Sri Lanka—A $3.5b 5-Year Programme," February 10, 2005.

*Economist* (US), "As Good as It Gets? Sri Lanka's Peace Process," October 16, 2004.

———, "Missed Chances; After the Tsunami," February 26, 2005.

———, "Still Squabbling: Sri Lanka," January 8, 2005.

Michael Elliott, "Sea of Sorrow: The World Suffers an Epic Tragedy as a Tsunami Spreads Death Across Asia," *Time,* January 10, 2005.

Bay Fang, "Keeping a War on Hold?" *U.S. News & World Report,* January 24, 2005.

Charlie Furniss, "Devoted to Conservation: Scientists in Sri Lanka Have Drawn Inspiration from History and Teamed Up with Buddhist Monks in an Attempt to Spread Environmental Awareness and to Put into Practice a Progressive Form of Forest Management," *Geographical,* February 2004.

Melinda Li, "Sri Lanka: Getting Relief to Tiger Territory," *Newsweek,* January 17, 2005.

Evan Thomas and George Wehrfritz, "Tide of Grief: The Earth Shrugged, and More than 140,000 Died," *Newsweek,* January 10, 2005.

*UPI NewsTrack,* "IMF Offers $157.5 Loan to Sri Lanka," March 4, 2005.

———, "Rebuilding Brings Brief Peace to Sri Lanka," January 4, 2005.

———, "Tamil Tiger Leader Killed in Sri Lanka," February 8, 2005.

*Xinhua News Agency*, "Sri Lanka Receives Half Million Tourists in 2003," January 2, 2004.

### INTERNET SOURCES

Angelfire, "The Story of Ceylon Tea." www.angelfire.com/wi/SriLanka/ceyl-tea.htm.

At Sri Lanka, "Ancient Cities—Anuradhapura," 2000. www.atsrilanka.com/anuradhapura.htm.

Bureau of Democracy, Human Rights, and Labor, U.S. Department of State, "Sri Lanka: International Religious Freedom Report," 2004. www.state.gov/g/drl/rls/irf/2004/35520.htm.

Bureau of South Asian Affairs, U.S. Department of State, "Background Note: Sri Lanka," February 2005. www.state.gov/r/pa/ei/bgn/5249.htm.

Nick Caraway, "Tsunami a Blessing in Disguise for Sri Lanka's Economy," Free Republic, February 8, 2005. www.freerepublic.com/focus/f-news/1338722/posts.

Center for International Development and Conflict Management, University of Maryland, "Assessment for Indian Tamils in Sri Lanka," 2004. www.cidcm.umd.edu/inscr/mar/assessment.asp?groupId=78001.

M.B. Dassanayake, "Dance and Music of the Sinhalese," Lanka Library. www.lankalibrary.com/rit/dance2.htm.

Economist, "Sri Lanka's Peace Process: As Good as It Gets?" October 14, 2004. www.economist.com/displayStory.cfm?story_id=3294801.

Efusion 1, "Handicrafts of Sri Lanka." http://efusion1.securesites.net/travel/lanka/art/handy.htm.

Sicille P.C. Kotelawala, "Classical Dances of Sri Lanka," Lanka Library. www.lankalibrary.com/rit/dance.htm.

Chandrika Kumaratunga, "Address to the Nation by Her Excellency the President on the 57th Anniversary of Independence," Presidents Sri Lanka, February 4, 2005. www.presidentsl.org/data/speech/2005/57th_independence_feb04.htm.

Lanka Library, "Sri Lanka: Food and Tropical Fruits," 2005. www.lankalibrary.com/food.shtml.

———, "Sri Lanka People and Ethnic Groups." www.lanka library.com/cul.html.

Alastair Lawson, "The Enigma of Prabhakaran," *BBC News*, May 2, 2000. http://news.bbc.co.uk/l/hi/world/south_ asia/212361.stm.

Living Heritage Trust of Sri Lanka, "Sri Pada: Myth, Legend, and Geography." http://sripada.org/index.htm.

Lonely Planet, "Destination Sri Lanka," 2004. www.lonely planet.com/destinations/indian_subcontinent/sri_lanka.

Nature Conservancy, "First Environmental Survey of Tsunami Damage Shows Sri Lankan Coasts and Forests Hurt but Rebounding," February 24, 2005. http://nature. org/pressroom/press/press1797.html.

Ozemail, "Stories of Elephants of Sri Lanka: Herds." http://members.ozemail.com.au/~cannont/HERDS.HTM.

Anoli Perera, "State of Sri Lankan Art," *Frontline*, February 13–26, 1999. www.flonnet.com/fl1604/16040660.htm.

Hemasiri Premawardene, "Dances of Sri Lanka," Lanka Library. www.lankalibrary.com/rit/dance2.htm.

Nadesan Satyendra, "New Delhi and the Tamil Struggle: The Indo Sri Lanka Agreement," Tamil Nation, January 1988. www.tamilnation.org/intframe/india/88saty.htm.

E.A. Selvanathan, "Has the Tamils' Struggle Ended?" *Green Left Weekly*, 1996. www.greenleft.org.au/back/1996/238/ 238p15.htm.

Kalinga Seneviratne, "The Plight of Sri Lankan Women," Third World Network. www.twnside.org.sg/title/plight-cn.htm.

Somini Sengupta, "Powerful Quake Jolts the Seabed off the West Coast of Indonesia," *New York Times*, March 29, 2005. www.nytimes.com.

Jasvinder Singh, "Tamil National Leader Hon. V. Pirapaharan's Interview," *Week Magazine* (India), March 3, 1986. www.eelamweb.com/leader.

Robert G. Smith, "Sri Lankan Music," Dr. Bob Smith Music Educator, February 18, 2005. http://members.iinet.net .au/~bobsmith/sri.htm.

South Asian Media Net, "People of Sri Lanka." www.southasian media.net/profile/srilanka/srilanka_people.cfm.

South Asian Terrorism Portal, "Suicide Killings—An Overview," 2001. www.satp.org/satporgtp/countries/shrilanka/data base/suicide_killings.htm.

Sri Lanka Tour, "Festivals in Sri Lanka," 2003. www.sri-lanka-tour.com/travel-guide/festivals.htm.

Tamil Nation, "Indictment Against Sri Lanka." www.tamil nation.org/srilankalaws/56sinhala.htm.

———, "Norwegian Peace Initiative: Proposal of the Liberation Tigers of Tamil Eelam on Behalf of the Tamil People for an Agreement to Establish an Interim Self Governing Authority for the North-East of the Island of Sri Lanka," November 1, 2003. www.tamilnation.org/conflictresolution/ tamileelam/norway/031101isga.htm.

Alisa Tang, "Tsunami Warning System Helped Spread Word," Associated Press, March 29, 2005. http://story.news. yahoo.com/news?tmpl=story&u=/ap/20050329/ap_on_ sc/tsunami_warn ing&cid=624&ncid=2360.

Travellers Worldwide, "About Columbo," November 5, 2004. www.travellersworldwide.com/09-srilanka/09-srilanka-about.htm.

Jayadeva Uyangoda, "Three Years After the Ceasefire Agreement: Where Have We Gone?" *Sri Lanka Daily Mirror*, March 16, 2005. www.tamilnation.org/conflictresolution/ tamileelam/norway/050316uyangoda.htm.

Vedda.org, "Sri Lanka's Vedda or Wanniyaleato." http:// vedda.org.

Young Asian Television, "Recover Sri Lanka," 2005. www. yatv.net/recoversl/index.htm.

# INDEX

Adam's Peak, 11, 13, 14
Almeida, Lourenço de, 26
animals, 18
Anuradhapura, 24, 26, 27, 33, 68
Arasanayagam, Jean, 74
architecture, 68–71
Aruvi Aru (river), 14
Asian elephants, 16
Aśoka (king), 24

Bambarakande Falls, 14
Bandaranaike, Sirimavo, 39, 40, 41
Bandaranaike, S.W.R.D., 8, 38–39
batik, 74
Bawa, Geoffrey, 71
beaches, 15, 17
beauty, 6, 11
biodiversity, 17–19
Blood, Peter R., 26, 30, 38
bo tree, 27
British, rule by, 6, 30–32, 33–35
Buddha, artwork related to, 71–72
Buddhism, 25, 32–33, 40, 56–57, 68, 77
    see also Anuradhapura
Buddhist chronicles, 24
Bullion, Alan J., 40, 44
Burghers, 55

Carraway, Nick, 82
caste system, 62–63
cease-fire, 47–49, 84, 88
central highlands, 11
Ceylon, 29
Ceylon Independence Act, 35
Ceylon National Congress, 34–35
Ceylon Tamil Congress, 36, 37
Ceylon Tamils, 52–53

Ceylon Workers' Congress, 43, 53
Chelvanayakam, S.J.V., 37, 39
Christianity, 57, 58
cities, 20–22
citizenship acts, 6, 8
civil war, 6, 8–9, 84–86
    see also cease-fire; ethnic con-
    flict
climate, 23
coastal zone, 12–13
coffee plantations, 30
Cōla empire, 26
Colombo, 20, 61, 72
constitution, 40, 45
coral reef habitats, 17
Corera, Alastair, 83
cricket, 66
crops, 12, 17, 19–20, 30–31
Crown Colony of Ceylon, 30, 32
cuisine, 75
Culavamsa, 24
culture, similarities of, among
    ethnic groups, 62–63
cyclones, 23

dagobas, 27
Dalada Maligawa (Temple of the
    Tooth), 22, 70
dance, 64–67
Daraniyagala, Justin, 72
Dayasheela, Herbert, 67
Devanampiya Tissa (king), 25
Dharmadasa, K.N.O., 43
Dissanayake, Gamini, 49
Diyaluma Falls, 14
drums, 67
dry zone, 12
Dutch, invasion by, 28–30
Dutch East India Company, 29

economy
  British rule and, 30
  civil war and, 49
  terrorism and, 44, 47
  tsunami and, 78–79, 82–84
education, 62
Elara, 26
elephants, 16
environmental damage, 18–19,
  81–82
ethnic conflict
  cease-fire in, 47–49, 84, 88
  Official Language Act and, 34
  peace accord of 1987, 44–46
  seeds of, 36–38
  SLFP government and, 38–39
  terrorism and violence, 43–44
  *see also* civil war
ethnic groups
  languages of, 58–59
  segregation of, 61
  similarities of culture among,
    62–63
  *see also specific groups*

Fang, Bay, 86
festivals, 76–77
folk dance, 67
folk religion, 64
folk songs, 67–68
forests, 17–19
43 Group, 72
Furniss, Charlie, 18

Gabriel, Richard, 72
Galle, 13, 20–21, 70
gemstones, 14
geography, 11–13
government system, 41–42
Gunesekera, Romesh, 74
Guttika, 26

handicrafts, 74–75
Heitzman, James, 51, 57, 61
Hikkaduwa, 15, 17
Hinduism, 58, 77
Hindu temples, 68–70

history
  ancient settlements and king-
    doms, 24–26
  British rule, 30–32
  Dutch invasion, 28–30
  nationalist movement, 32–35
  Portuguese settlers, 26–28
hydroelectric power, 14

independence, 6, 35
India, 9, 44–46
Indian Tamils, 52–54
  citizenship of, 36–37
indigenous people, 55–56
International Monetary Fund, 80
Islam, 54–55, 58, 77

Jaffna, 22
Jaffna Peninsula, 12, 17
Janatha Vimukthi Peramuna. *See*
  People's Liberation Front
Java, 28–29
Jayasinghe, Susanthika, 66
Jayewardene, J.R., 8, 41–42, 44
Jeffries, Charles, 6, 13, 32
jewelry, 74–75

Kalu (river), 14
Kandy, 21–22, 50
Kandyan dance, 64–65
Kelani (river), 14
Keyt, George, 72
Kumaratunga, Chandrika
  cease-fire and, 9
  coalition party of, 89
  LTTE and, 42
  as president, 47, 48–49
  prime ministers and, 87–88
  Tamil insurgency and, 86–87
  tsunami and, 79, 80, 84–85

Land Reform Act, 31
language
  of ethnic groups, 58–59
  Jayewardene government and,
    43
  literature and, 72–73

politics and, 59–60
of Tamils, 40
*see also* Official Language Act
Legislative Council, 33, 34–35
Liberation Tigers of Tamil Eelam
 (LTTE)
 cease-fire and, 9
 Indian Peace-Keeping Force
 and, 46
 interim proposal by, 85, 86
 leader of, 53
 negotiations with, 48–49
 power struggles within, 84
 terrorism of, 8, 42, 43, 47
 tsunami recovery and, 79
literature, 72–74

macaques, 19
Maduru Oya National Park, 56
*Mahavamsa*, 24, 73
Mahaweli (river), 14
Mahinda, (prince), 25
Malays, 54–55
Mannar Island, 12–13
marine resources, 15
masks, 74
McGowen, William, 47
media, 73
middle class, growth of, 32
monsoon winds, 23
Moors, 54
mountains, 11, 13
music, 67–68
Muslims, 54–55, 58, 77

Nallur Kandaswamy Temple, 69,
 70
Namunakuli, 11
National Art Gallery, 72
nationalist movement, 32–35
nature sanctuaries, 18–19
New Year festival, 77
Nias, 22

Official Language Act, 8, 34, 39
Ondaatje, Michael, 74
Operation Sunshine, 48, 49

paintings, 71–72
Pandukabhaya (king), 24
Parakramabahu I, VI, and VIII
 (kings), 26
peace, prospects for, 8–9, 84–86
peace accord of 1987, 44–46
People's Alliance, 48
People's Liberation Front (JVP),
 9, 46–47, 89
Perera, Anoli, 72
Peries, Ivan, 72
Pidurutalagala, 11
pilgrimage, 13
plains, 12
plantation system, 30
politics
 language and, 59–60
 uncertainty in, 86–89
Polonnaruwa, 26, 33
Ponnambalam, G.G., 36
Poothanthevanar, Eelattu, 73
population, 20, 38, 50–54
 *see also* ethnic groups
Portuguese, 26–29
Prabhakaran, Velupillai, 53, 84
Premadasa, Ranasinghe, 42,
 47–48
Premawardene, Hemasiri, 64
president, 41–42
Prevention of Terrorism Act, 43

rain forests, 17–18
Rajapakse, Mahinda, 88
*Ramayana*, 24
Ranasinghe, Ann, 74
reefs, coral, 17
reforms, under British rule, 31–32
refugee camps, 54
religion, 54–55, 56–58, 77
 *see also* Buddhism
riots, 39, 43–44
rivers, 13–14
rubber, 31
Ruhunu dance, 65–66

Sabaragamuwa dance, 66
Sanjayan, M.A., 81–82

Satyendra, Nadesan, 46
sculpture, 71
segregation, of ethnic groups, 61
Selvadurai, Shyam, 74
Sena, 26
Senanayake, Don Stephan, 35,
    36–38
Senanayake, Dudley, 38
settlements, 19–20
Sinha (king), 24
Sinhalese
    Anuradhapura and, 27
    Buddhism and, 32–33
    civil war and, 6, 8–9
    history of, 24–26
    Official Language Act and, 34
    population of, 50–51
    Portuguese and, 27–28
    SLFP government and, 38–39
Sinharaja Forest, 17
Smith, Robert G., 67
Solheim, Erik, 49
spices, 27, 28–29
sports, 66
Sri Jayawardenepura, 20
Sri Lanka Freedom Party (SLFP),
    38–39
suicide attacks, 42

Tamil Federal Party, 37
Tamil Language Regulations, 40
Tamils
    aid distribution and, 85–86
    cities of, 22
    civil war and, 6, 8–9
    dances of, 66–67
    discrimination against, 40, 43
    history of, 25–26
    language of, 40
    Official Language Act and, 34

plantation system and, 30, 31
population of, 51–54
see also Ceylon Tamils; Indian
    Tamils; Liberation Tigers of
    Tamil Eelam
Tamil United Liberation Front
    (TULF), 40–41, 42–43
teas, 12, 31
terrorism, 42, 43, 44
Thamilchelvam, Suppah
    Paramu, 84–85
Thuparama Dagoba, 25
tourism, 15, 17, 78–79
Trincomalee, 13, 15, 22
tsunami, 10, 22–23
    economy and, 82–84
    environmental damage and,
        81–82
    ethnic tensions since, 85–86
    recovery from, 78–81

United Front, 40
United National Party (UNP), 35,
    36, 38, 40, 41
United People's Freedom Al-
    liance, 89
university, education at, 62
Uyangoda, Jayadeva, 88

Veddas, 55–56
Vijaya (prince), 24
violence, ethnic, 43–44

waterfalls, 14
Wickramasinghe, Martin, 73
Wickremesinghe, Ranil, 87–88
Williams, Harry, 13
Wilson, A. Jeyaratnam, 48
women, status of, 59

# PICTURE CREDITS

# About the Author

Debra A. Miller is a writer and lawyer with a passion for current events and history. She began her law career in Washington, D.C., where she worked on policy and legal matters in government, public interest, and private law-firm positions. She now lives with her husband in Encinitas, California. She has written and edited publications for legal publishers, as well as numerous books and anthologies on historical and political topics.